Published in Columbia, South Carolina,
during the one hundred and seventy-fifth anniversary
of the establishment
of the University of South Carolina
and the two hundredth anniversary
of the establishment of the
United States of America.

The Public Treasury
of Colonial South Carolina

TRICENTENNIAL STUDIES, NUMBER 10

This volume is part of a series of *Tricentennial Studies,* published by the University of South Carolina Press on behalf of the South Carolina Tricentennial Commission, to commemorate the founding of South Carolina in 1670.

THE PUBLIC TREASURY OF COLONIAL SOUTH CAROLINA

by Maurice A. Crouse

Published for the
South Carolina Tricentennial Commission
by the
UNIVERSITY OF SOUTH CAROLINA PRESS
Columbia, South Carolina

Copyright © University of South Carolina 1977

FIRST EDITION

Published in Columbia, S.C., by the
University of South Carolina Press, 1977
Manufactured in the United States of America

Library of Congress Cataloging in Publication Data
Crouse, Maurice A
    The Public Treasury of colonial South Carolina.
    (Tricentennial studies; no. 10)
    Bibliography: p.
    Includes index.
    1.   South Carolina (Colony). Public Treasury.
2.   Finance, Public—South Carolina—History.
I.   Title. II.   Series: South Carolina Tricen-
tennial Commission. Tricentennial studies; no. 10.
HJ687.C76   336.757   76-56125
ISBN 0-87249-255-9

For all my family

CONTENTS

LIST OF TABLES

PREFACE

A FRIEND OF MINE who has written about the Confederate Congresses once remarked to me that he did not wish to become typed as a Southern historian. Similarly, though I have written about the Public Treasury of South Carolina, I do not wish to become typed as an economic historian. I certainly did not intend to become one when I accepted the suggestion of Professor Clarence L. Ver Steeg of Northwestern University that I write my dissertation on the Manigault family, but one thing led to another. Because Gabriel Manigault was public treasurer from 1735 to 1743, I learned much about the Treasury's operations during that period. Because no one else has ever done the task, I was asked by the South Carolina Tricentennial Commission to broaden my investigations to produce the present work.

Many persons and institutions have assisted me. Professor George C. Rogers of the University of South Carolina has been a never-failing source of help by suggesting improvements in my manuscript, and he has transmitted to me suggestions made by others, particularly Professor Robert M. Weir. I owe much to Miss Cynthia J. Hawes, who wrote a master's thesis under my direction at Memphis State University on the revenue offices in South Carolina before 1735; her work guided my own in this early period. The provincial records housed in the South Carolina Department of Archives and History were essential to my work. Director Charles Lee often went out of his way to help me with them, as did many members of his staff, particularly Miss Wylma Wates, Miss Ruth Green, and Mr. William McDowell. I also received considerable assistance from Mr. E.L. Inabinett and the

South Caroliniana Library, Mrs. Granville T. Prior and the South
Carolina Historical Society, and Mr. Lester Pourciau and the John
W. Brister Library of Memphis State University.

NOTE ON STYLE

I have reproduced quotations from printed sources as printed
(although some printed editions do not follow the original manuscripts exactly), except that I have brought superior letters down
into the line of text and I have spelled out a few contractions
represented by special characters which are not easily reproduced. In quotations from manuscript sources, the only change
that I have made is to bring superior letters down into the line of
text.

For citing references to the journals of the Commons House
and Council, I have chosen a system that should allow location of
the material in any of the various forms in which the journals may
be found. I give first the kind of journal and the date of the entry
(which are common to all the forms), then a reference to the
volume, classification, or other numbers peculiar to the cited
source.

Wherever they are available I have chosen to cite published
editions of the journals, which the reader may find more accessi-
ble and certainly easier to read than the originals or microfilm
copies. A typical entry is "Commons House Journal, October 7,
1737, *JCH*, *1736–1739*, 341," which is a shortened reference to
*Colonial Records of South Carolina: The Journal of the Commons House
of Assembly, November 10, 1736–June 7, 1739*, ed. J.H. Easterby
(Columbia, 1951), in which the journal entry for October 7, 1737,
will be found on page 341. Because of the great length of the titles
of the published journals, I shall use the shortened form for
subsequent citations.

Where there has been no publication, I have generally used the
"fair copy" journals in the South Carolina Department of Archives and History. For example, "Council Journal, February 4,
1737/8, VII, 65" refers to the fair copy of the Council journals,
where an entry for February 4, 1737/8, will be found on page 65

of the seventh volume. There is one peculiarity which should be noted. The journals of the Council recorded when it sat as the Upper House of Assembly are often contained in volumes which now bear the designation of "Council Journal." It is sometimes necessary, therefore, to have a reference such as "Upper House Journal, April 4, 1739, CJ, vii, 201–2." (Except in citations, I shall for simplicity's sake use the title "Council" for the body sitting either as Council or as upper house.)

Copies of the journals were sent during colonial times to the Board of Trade, and those which are now in the British Public Record Office may be used to fill gaps in the Archives' series. A typical entry of this sort is "Commons House Journal, April 3, 1772, C.O. 5/478, 3–4," which refers to the Public Record Office's category for the American colonies and document number 478 within it.

Dates are always those given in the documents themselves, except that for dates between January 1 and March 24, inclusive, before 1753, I have indicated both Old Style and New Style years where the document has not already done so. For example, "February 23, 1722," has been adjusted to read "February 23, 1722/3." I have made no adjustment for the number of days that the Old Style calendar lagged behind the current one.

Amounts of money are often designated as sterling, proclamation money, South Carolina currency, or other units. Where there is no designation, the amount is to be understood as South Carolina currency.

I have chosen to proceed topically for the most part rather than chronologically. I have also attempted to make each chapter stand alone, as well as it may. Sometimes I have been able to accomplish this purpose by cross-references to other chapters, but at other times a certain amount of repetition has been, in my judgment, unavoidable. I trust that the reader will look charitably upon the repetition when he realizes that the alternative would have been the weaving of a half-dozen or so topical threads into a single, integrated, but impossibly complex, narrative.

Maurice A. Crouse
December 1975

CHAPTER I

Origins and Functions

THE PUBLIC TREASURY OF SOUTH CAROLINA came into being as a result of the duty act of 1691, which levied duties on furs and skins exported from the province and appointed Jonathan Amory as public receiver to handle the funds.[1] Import duties were soon added to supplement the original export duties, and the duty acts always specified that the public receiver (later called the public treasurer) should be responsible and accountable for the duty funds. The regular tax acts also routinely appointed the public treasurer as the custodian of tax funds. These duties and taxes constituted by far the greater part of the moneys entrusted to the public treasurer, but he also received small sums from licenses for tavernkeepers, peddlers, and Indian traders; fines, forfeitures, and seizures for violation of the provincial customs laws; and possibly other sources. As a matter of convenience, he came to be the custodian and disbursing agent of nearly all the public funds.

The public treasurer handled only the funds generated by acts of the General Assembly, and he was solely the assembly's agent— he in no way received authority from, nor was he answerable to, any power outside the province.[2] During both the proprietary and royal periods there were other funds which were raised by authority of the proprietors, the king, or parliament and which were handled by other officials. The proprietors, for example, appointed their own official, called the receiver-general, to receive the payment of quitrents, and when South Carolina became a royal province in 1721 the Crown appointed a receiver-general of the quitrents.[3] The collection of parliamentary customs duties, such as the Molasses Act of 1733, was handled entirely separately from the Public Treasury. These were therefore not "public" funds, for the elected representatives of the people had no direct role in levying and appropriating them nor in controlling the officials administering them. Since they did not ordinarily enter into the Public Treasury, these funds are not dealt with in this study.

BONDS AND OATHS

Before the public treasurer entered his office, he had to post a bond guaranteeing the faithful execution of the duties of his office and to take various oaths. A bond was required of Thomas Smith in 1700,[4] and may have been required of the earlier office holders, but the duty act of 1703 was the first extant act to mention the formal requirement that £3,000 be posted. Possibly because of depreciation of the currency, the amount of the bond was raised to £6,000 in 1707, but it was reduced to £5,000 in 1711 and stayed at that level until the end of the proprietary period. During most of the royal period the amount of the bond was £7,000 sterling. In 1771 it was set at £40,000 proclamation money, or £30,000 sterling, for each of the joint public treasurers. The primary reason for the high bond was doubtless the concern of royal officials that the public treasurers obey the additional instruction which was issued as a result of the Wilkes fund controversy.[5] But the fact that the previous public treasurer, Jacob Motte, had twice incurred very large deficits may have also been a consideration. It was customary at first for the bond to be held in the office of the secretary of the province, but after 1721 another copy of the bond was deposited with the speaker or clerk of the Commons House, possibly as a symbol of that body's special association with the public treasurer.[6]

In addition to posting bond, the public treasurer customarily "took the Oaths, Subscribed the Test and took the Oath of Office."[7] Only the oath of office and a minor oath relating to the drawing of jury lists seem to have been prescribed by provincial law, but the language used above indicates that the public treasurer also took the oaths required of any British office holder after the time of Queen Anne, including an oath of allegiance to the Crown, the oath of supremacy, an oath of abjuration of the Pretender, and a declaration against transubstantiation.[8] During the royal period the public treasurer swore as his oath of office that

> I, A B, appointed treasurer of the Province of South Carolina, will truly and faithfully discharge the trust reposed in me as treasurer of the same; I will not issue, dispose, or apply, or cause to be issued, disposed, or applyed, any money that may hereafter come into my hands as treasurer aforesaid, otherwise than is or shall be directed by this or any other Act or Acts, or written orders of the General Assembly of this Province, and I will keep true and faithful accounts of all the moneys or effects that is or may come into my hands or possession, and that shall be issued and paid by me, by virtue of any such Acts or orders, with times of my receiving and paying the same, so help me God.[9]

KEEPING THE RECORDS

There is little evidence as to how the public treasurer went about doing his work except that provided by the financial journals and ledgers and the legislative journals. It is known that he was expected to keep regular office hours for the benefit of those who had duties to pay. The early acts do not specify the location, but the public receiver was required to be present with the comptroller (a lesser revenue official) at their office from nine until twelve o'clock daily except Sundays and holidays.[10] An act of 1771 stated that as soon as the new exchange and custom house were finished, the office of the public treasurer would be the large room over the guard house and the two rooms adjoining.[11]

It is uncertain where the funds of the Public Treasury were actually located. It seems likely from the evidence available that much of the time the Treasury operated as a bookkeeping center, with "paper credits" and "paper debits," the actual money being loaned out or otherwise in use. At other times, though, storage facilities definitely were necessary. In 1748 the Commons House authorized Jacob Motte to purchase an "iron Chest for the Use of the Treasury...."[12]

The chief source of information about the operation of the Public Treasury is the collection of journals and ledgers prepared by that office. The surviving Treasury records are substantial but not complete. They include a "ledger" kept by Alexander Parris for the years 1725–1730; three journals labeled "Journal A: Duties, 1735, 1748," "Journal B: Duties, 1748–1765," and "Journal C: Duties, 1765–1776"; two ledgers labeled "Ledger B: Accounts Approved, 1735–1773" and "Publick's Ledger, 1771–1776"; and a record of general tax receipts and payments for the period 1761–1771.[13]

With the exception of Parris's ledger, the books are all finished products and represent the compilation and editing of rough copies or "waste books" that have perished. It is likely that Parris's ledger was meant as a final copy too, for Parris was known for being a sloppy record keeper.[14] The ledger is apparently the third in a series of four[15] and is really a combination journal and ledger, containing a detailed listing of all cash received as well as summary accounts. All the other records kept by Parris have apparently disappeared. In fact, it was reported in 1744 that *all* the Treasury records before 1735 had been "burnt, or otherwise destroyed. . . ."[16] At any rate, the continuous series of records begins with Gabriel Manigault's assumption of the office of public treasurer in 1735. Interestingly, Manigault's books open with no balances carried forward from Parris's accounts. Probably Parris's records were in such confusion that no meaningful balances could be determined at the time.

It was the practice of the public treasurer to keep in a journal a running account of all duties received from the various duties which were collected and a similar running account of all disbursements from each duty fund. Every six months the activities would be summarized in a ledger account for each fund, and a cash account would be prepared to give an overall summary. In accordance with English tradition, the accounts were prepared on September 29 (Michaelmas Day), which was mid-year according to the Old Style calendar, and on March 25 (Lady Day), the beginning of the new year. Although South Carolina adopted the New Style calendar in 1752 along with the rest of the British

Empire, the Treasury continued to keep its duty records on the basis of the old calendar until 1768, when the accounting period was closed on December 31. (Supplementary balances were prepared June 18, 1770, when Jacob Motte died; February 26, 1771, when Henry Peronneau and Benjamin Dart became joint public treasurers; and March 4, 1776, when the commissioners of the Treasury made an audit for the Provincial Congress.)

Some of the public treasurers were far from perfect bookkeepers. If one examines the Treasury records, it is easy to see why errors could occur. The accounts at first glance give the semblance of double-entry bookkeeping, but the safeguards of such a system are lacking. The all-important cash account did not receive an entry every time an entry was made in the other accounts; it was itself a summary of the total receipts and disbursements of the other accounts and therefore offered no independent check upon their accuracy. Jacob Motte made so many errors that at one time his cash account showed £19,318 8s 11d more than was actually in the treasury, and on another occasion, because he forgot to deduct various charges, his records showed £74,082 8s 10d more than he had in hand.[17] Even the otherwise meticulous Gabriel Manigault made an error, which apparently no one detected at the time, in carrying forward a cash balance.[18]

Evidently the accounts of the public treasurer were largely *pro forma*. That is, they represented how the various funds *should* stand at any given time, but it is fairly apparent that the *actual* standing could be quite different. For example, individual accounts could incur huge deficits for several accounting periods in succession before a bookkeeping entry would be made to transfer money from other accounts to bring them into balance. (In the meantime, disbursements must actually have come from the other accounts.) Henry Peronneau reported in August 1773 that there was barely £10,000 in the Treasury and that he feared bankruptcy, although his cash account of December 31, 1772, had showed a balance of £79,039 11s 11d and it was to increase to £133,133 6s 4d by the end of 1773. The trouble was that most of the "cash" consisted of merchants' bonds for duties which they could not pay.[19] The Treasury even operated on cash deficits at times, meaning that the entire resources of the Treasury had been overdrawn and funds from private sources were being used. The cash account was short £10,502 6s 4d in September 1757. The deficit increased to £21,733 4s 4d by March 1758, and there would have been a much worse deficit for the next accounting period if the issue of £62,300 in public orders (a form of paper money) had not been entered as income. Even then, the Treasury had sunk £3,726 14s 9½d into the red by March 1759 before recovering. To help maintain the solvency of the Treasury, John Savage led a campaign to secure loans from Charles Town merchants which resulted in £45,000 being advanced by nine important merchants or firms. In March 1768 the Treasury showed a deficit of £13,771 11s 7d, and in February 1771 it incurred the greatest deficit in its history: £25,495 13s 3d.[20]

The account of the fund for building a state house is a very clear example of *pro forma* bookkeeping. The public treasurer disbursed £44,500 from the account before September 29, 1758, but he had received only £18,229 3s 4d by that time. It took until September 29, 1766, for the fund to receive enough bookkeeping credits from the general duty fund to be brought into "balance." Similarly, the fund for St. Michael's church had received only £4,187 10s before March 25, 1754, but some £15,000 had been "paid out." It was September 29, 1761, before the account was "balanced" by transfers.[21] It is obvious that the accounts were mere bookkeeping entries to show from what source the funds had been collected (or were to be collected in the future) and from which the money had in theory been paid out.

It is a peculiarity of the records of the public treasurer that in the early years they never contained accounts unless they were funded from the import or export duties. That other accounts were kept is known from the frequent references to them in the journals of the Commons house, so an entire body of Treasury records probably has perished. The accounts of the public orders of 1736/7 have survived in some detail,[22] as have occasional records of the town watch fund.[23] Committees reported examining accounts of the sale of Negro slaves employed at the silk works, interest on bonds and notes received for duties on Negroes, fines and forfeitures received from the clerk of the Crown,[24] and moneys received for making gun carriages and for building the barracks at Fort Johnson.[25] The pattern was not always followed. In the 1750s Jacob Motte entered in his ledger several accounts that drew their financing solely from the general tax acts, such as the accounts for a magazine at Dorchester and for fortifications at Fort Johnson and Port Royal.[26] The rationale for their inclusion might be that they were funds appropriated in advance of the actual expenditures, rather than payments of charges already incurred, as was ordinarily true of items financed through direct taxation.

AUTHORITY FOR COLLECTIONS AND DISBURSEMENTS

In one sense, the public treasurer was little more than a bookkeeper. It should be clearly understood that he was not a policy maker but entirely the servant of the Assembly. Although the Assembly might call upon him for his expert opinion and advice, it reserved to itself the power of decision, and the public treasurer was expected to follow its directives. He was strictly accountable to the Assembly for his actions, for that body eventually approved or disapproved all his accounts and held him responsible for all the funds entrusted to him. It is perhaps not stretching the point to say that the perfect public treasurer would have been a robot, exactly obeying the wishes of the Assembly.

The public treasurer collected moneys by the authority given him by the various duty and tax laws passed by the Assembly. His authority to pay out funds came from four or five different sources: the annual appropriations act, a specific order of the Assembly, an order of the governor-in-council, the countersignature of a responsible official, or his own initiative.

Perhaps most important was the authority of the annual appropriations act, which specified literally to the last farthing how the appropriated funds were to be disbursed. After 1733 the act was passed to pay for charges already incurred rather than for those which were anticipated. Creditors of the government were required to turn in accounts to the Assembly, where they were scrutinized for validity and accuracy, and if allowed, the accounts were placed in a schedule attached to the tax act. The public treasurer was then authorized to issue certificates of indebtedness for those amounts to the creditors. These certificates were receivable in payment of taxes and duties and would be canceled when so returned to the treasury.[27]

The public treasurer might disburse funds as a result of a specific order of the Assembly. For example, in February 1740/1, the commissioners appointed for building St. Philip's Church petitioned the Assembly for a sum of money to buy some land for the churchyard. Upon a favorable hearing of the petition, the Commons House passed the following resolution:

> Resolved, that Gabriel Manigault Esq. the Public Treasurer of this Province, do pay the Sum of £1,300:00:00 to the Commissioners for building the Brick Church in Charles Town, to enable them to purchase certain Lands belonging to John Milner and Zachariah Carlile their Heirs or Devisees for the Use of the Church and Church Yard, out of the Sum of £1,600:00:00 provided by the Act for laying a Duty on Rum imported, now lying in the said Public Treasurer's Hands pursuant to the Prayer of the Memorial of the said Commissioners....[28]

This resolution illustrates how closely control of spending was retained by the Assembly. Not only was the amount specified, but so was the particular fund from which it was to be paid. In the early years an order such as this was always sent up to the Council and Governor for their concurrence, a procedure not necessarily followed in the later colonial period.[29]

The governor-in-council might authorize disbursements, as he did in February 1742/3, when Manigault was directed to pay Othniel Beale £1,500 out of the fund for the relief of Georgia, to be used for paying overseers and hiring Negroes to work on the town's fortifications.[30] However, the Commons House still had to approve the public treasurer's account of such orders, and it occasionally challenged the right of the governor-in-council to direct disbursements.[31]

The public treasurer might also disburse funds upon the order of a responsible official such as the commissary-general, who in turn derived his authority from an act or order of the Assembly. In effect, the public treasurer was then acting as custodian of funds already allotted and needed no further warrant from the Assembly. Typical of this arrangement was an order issued by the Commons House in 1738, creating a fund of £1,000 against which John Dart, the commissary-general, could draw.[32]

Finally, the public treasurer could spend incidental sums on his own initiative. The Assembly always had an effective check on this, however, for the public treasurer was required to submit an account of all such expenditures. The legislative journals seldom give much detailed information about these accounts. One of Gabriel Manigault's accounts covering the period from March 29, 1740, to January 31, 1740/1, is extant, however. An account for £1,648, it is also noted in the journal of the Commons House for February 19, 1740/1. It lists £55 2s 6d for repairs to the state house; £29 17s 6d for expenses of the council chamber, including firewood and candles; £6 5s for a counterfeit public order used to convict a forger; £64 for printing and forms; and £1,491 15s for various orders of the lieutenant governor.[33] If this account is typical, the public treasurer's initiative was rather restricted. He could disburse moneys for only the smallest sums without fear of being disallowed by the Commons House. He could afford to take greater chances by paying orders of the governor or lieutenant governor, for he could usually depend on the Council to support those officials against any action by the Commons House. That Lieutenant Governor Thomas Broughton was Manigault's brother-in-law probably helped, too.

So closely was the public treasurer restrained by the Assembly that he could not make simple decisions that today would be regarded as merely administrative. The remission of duties on slaves not intended for resale for profit is a case in point. In order to secure the remission of a duty that might be as little as £5, the importer had to petition the Assembly. The Assembly as a rule granted the remission upon the condition that the importer give bond that the slave or slaves were intended for his own use and would not be sold within a certain period after their entry. This procedure apparently had to be followed for each and every remission—the public treasurer did not have the authority to decide the matter for himself.[34]

THE PUBLIC TREASURER'S HELPERS

The public treasurer did not work alone; he had a number of lesser officials assisting him in the performance of his duties. During part of the proprietary period, it seems to have been the practice for the public receiver to have had a deputy, for such an official is often referred to in the statutes and in legislative journals. The deputy was authorized to perform the same duties as the public receiver, though only if the latter were not present.[35] Ordinarily the deputy was appointed by the Assembly, but the public receiver could in time of emergency appoint his own deputy.[36] The position seems to have disappeared during the royal period, but it is likely that the functions were carried on by the various clerks employed in the public treasurer's office. During the years of his illness, Jacob Motte employed Henry Peronneau as his assistant and allowed him to perform virtually all the work of the office.[37]

Working very closely with the public treasurer was the comptroller, whose office was created by an act of 1703.[38] It was he rather than the public receiver or public treasurer himself, who actually dealt with the collection of duties and the associated tasks of maintaining port records and receiving declarations of cargo.[39] Beginning in 1736, both the public treasurer and the comptroller were authorized to appoint deputies in Port Royal (Beaufort) and George Town.[40] Under their direction also were the lesser port officials, generally two men who filled the positions of waiters, gaugers, and searchers. The titles of the officials are indicative of their multiple functions. As waiters they would "wait" aboard vessels to make sure that no loading or unloading of goods took place until they received certification from the comptroller and public receiver that the required duties had been paid. As gaugers they helped in ascertaining the contents of containers and in making estimates of weights and measures of goods. As searchers they searched vessels or buildings to make sure that no goods were concealed to avoid payment of duties. Really jacks-of-all-trades, the waiters, gaugers, and searchers did whatever they were directed by their superiors. They were appointed by the Assembly, but the public receiver and comptroller had the right to make interim appointments, subject to the Assembly's ratification.[41]

In the collection of the annual tax the public treasurer was assisted by inquirers, assessors, and collectors, all of whom were appointed by the tax act itself. The inquirers made a survey of all taxable property owned by each individual within their districts. The assessors used the lists as a basis for prorating the levies, and the collectors collected the sums due.[42]

THE PUBLIC TREASURER'S CONCURRENT DUTIES

Although the public treasurer had assistance from various officials in the performance of his own duties, it was not unusual during the proprietary period and for the first years of the royal period for him to serve concurrently in other high offices. Jonathan Amory, the first public treasurer, was also Speaker of the Commons House during the years 1692–93 and 1696–99.[43] He seems to have also been attorney-general and advocate of the court of vice-admiralty around 1697 and 1698.[44]

The combining of the offices of public treasurer and speaker of the Commons House suggests the arrangement under which John Robinson achieved considerable power in Virginia,[45] but Amory did not hold the offices long enough to secure similar power. After 1721 members of both the Commons House and the Council were prohibited by law from being public treasurer during their tenure as legislators, so there was no possibility of such an arrangement.[46]

The closest parallel to John Robinson was Alexander Parris, who during much of his long tenure as public treasurer served also as commissary-general. If Governor James Glen is to be believed (and there is little to suggest that he should), Parris exercised considerable influence over the Assembly.[47] Even before the official establishment of the office, there were activities of the public receiver which indicate that he may already have been serving as a kind of commissary-general to procure supplies for the military forces.[48] The statute which appointed the first commissary-general has not been located, but in 1723 a statute authorized the public treasurer to provide for the frontier garrisons,[49] and in the estimate for that year's tax bill Alexander Parris was granted a salary for acting as commissary-general, over and above the remuneration which he received as public treasurer.[50]

After 1731 a major part of the work of the commissary-general was to provide for the settlement of poor Protestant immigrants in the backcountry settlements which were proposed by Governor Robert Johnson.[51] It was Johnson's opinion that the extra work involved in the position made its combination with that of public treasurer unwise, and even before the Assembly voted to remove Parris from the Treasury for malfeasance, Johnson had already proposed that a separate commissary-general be appointed. Captain Peter Taylor replaced Parris in that office.[52] In justifying the separation of the two offices, Johnson mentioned only the work involved, so it is doubtful that Parris had actually exercised any great political powers. Indeed, the close control which the Commons House had over both offices would tend to rule out any accumulation of power by the holders.

One of the minor tasks associated with the position of public treasurer was that of helping prepare the lists of persons who were eligible to serve on the grand jury, the petit juries, and special juries. Because the jury lists were drawn up on the basis of taxes paid by individuals, it was only natural that the public treasurer should assist.[53]

The public treasurer also had the constantly vexing problem of collecting license fees from tavern keepers and others who sold "strong liquor." These persons were actually licensed by the justices of the peace, but the license was not valid until the fees had been paid. As Gabriel Manigault's stern advertisements show, the sellers were anything but punctual about paying and had to be threatened with prosecution before they complied.[54] Indian traders seem to have been more tractable about paying their fees. At any rate, Manigault did not publish threatening advertisements about them.[55]

The public treasurer had also to inquire every month about the prices of various kinds of flour and publish a table showing the legal weights of loaves of bread, in accordance with the law on the assize of bread,[56] though it is difficult to see why this task should have fallen to him.

It was one of the incongruities of his office that although he had to perform such miscellaneous tasks, the public treasurer was not necessarily involved in all matters of finance. He was technically only the custodian of funds, and if he participated in policy decisions or rendered other services, it was probably because of his personal qualifications or for the sake of convenience. Gabriel Manigault served, for example, on the commission of 1735 to exchange the old currency bills which had been extensively counterfeited.[57] That he did so not in his capacity as public treasurer but as a private citizen is indicated by his receiving special compensation.[58] Although the public orders, a type of bill of credit, were issued through his office, the public treasurer was ordinarily not a commissioner for the issues.

COMPENSATION

The compensation which the public treasurer received for his services changed considerably over the years. At times he received a commission on the amounts he handled; at others he was paid a flat salary regardless of the amounts. The duty law of 1691 allowed him 10 percent of everything he collected or paid out.[59] Beginning in 1706, George Logan was allowed 5 percent for receiving, 2½ percent for paying out.[60] In 1707 the system was changed to a salary of £150 annually "in lieu of all fees, dues and perquisites."[61] Because of the depreciation of the currency and the heavier work, the salary was increased to £400 annually in 1717.[62] Just before the end of the proprietary period there was a reversion to the commission system: the public receiver was to receive 5 percent on all moneys received and 2½ percent on all moneys disbursed, plus fees of 2s 6d for each entry in his books and 5s for each certificate of clearance which he issued.[63] The commissions remained at this level until 1740, when the general duty act reduced the commission on receipts to 2½ percent, possibly as an austerity move to cut expenses, or possibly as a reflection of feeling that the public treasurer was overpaid.[64]

The fees became rather diversified. At one time, for every entry in the general duty, fortifications, and rum accounts, the public treasurer received 6d. For every entry for Negroes he received 2s, and for each entry of deerskins and sole leather exported, 1s. For every drawback, or refund of import duties when goods were re-exported, the public treasurer was entitled to 1s; for every clearance of vessels and manifest, 2s; and for every bond and license for retailing liquors, 4s.[65]

His income from fees is not known, but it does not appear to have been great.[66] Until the commission schedule was changed in 1740, Gabriel Manigault received between £2,329 6s 2d and £3,271 15s 9d each year. The reduction of the commission on recipts caused his income to fall to about one-half that level during the remainder of his term as public treasurer (until 1743). The cash accounts of the Treasury thereafter indicate that commissions generally did not go above £1,500 per year until the middle of the 1750s. Then, because of the greater spending caused by the French and Indian War, the commissions began getting larger, reaching a peak at £3,332 4s 7d in 1758. The return of peace caused the public treasurer no loss of commissions, however. The province began a series of costly building programs, including the erection of a new exchange and customs house, a new watch house, a poor house, a hospital, and courthouses and jails in the backcountry. The account for new settlers was especially active. As a result, the public treasurer was making more money than ever before. Commissions usually amounted to more than £3,000 per year, and in 1771 the joint public treasurers divided £5,378 3s 1d between them.[67]

The public treasurer received nothing for handling the accounts of the annual tax. Only the collectors received commissions, although at least one public treasurer protested the unfairness of such work without any reward.[68] Nor does it appear that the public treasurer received much allowance for clerical assistance. In 1737 the Commons House at first refused to give any allowance for clerks but finally did provide £200.[69] It refused in

1745 to make payment for copies of the treasury books, maintaining that the furnishing of copies was a normal function of the office.[70]

One controversy about the compensation of the public treasurer seems to have faded away without being resolved. When Gabriel Manigault left the office in 1743, the Commons House refused to allow him commissions on the transfer of funds to the new public treasurer, Jacob Motte, although a committee recommended that it consider commissions on certain sums.[71] Whether out of sympathy with Manigault or simply to pick a quarrel with the Commons House, the Council rejected the settlement, saying that Manigault could not possibly comply. It was noted that Manigault accepted the resolution that no commissions be allowed on the transfer of funds to Motte. This, however, opened up a new claim. Motte would presumably be allowed commissions upon paying out the funds. Manigault had received £14,189 5s 7d from Parris after entering the office in 1735 and had taken no commissions upon paying out the funds. It was argued that his was exactly the same case as Motte's. The committee of the Council recommended the consideration of all these claims, as well as commissions on a sum loaned from the fortifications duty fund to the commissioners of the curtain line.[72] The disagreement between the two houses seems to have died, though as late as May 1745, the Council was still insisting that the public treasurer's books could not be settled by an order of either house of the Assembly alone.[73] But nothing more was heard, and there is no record that any adjustment was ever made.

A very large portion of the public treasurer's income was "hidden" because it was not specified in the appointing statutes and was not paid from the Treasury itself. The public treasurer had the privilege of putting out public money at interest as long as there was no immediate call for it, and the interest could be retained by him as personal income. (In 1773 both the Commons House and the Council attempted to remove the interest advantage, but apparently did not succeed.)[74] When Henry Peronneau appeared in 1784 before the board which was considering Loyalist claims, it was agreed by all the witnesses that the receiving of interest created more income than did the commissions. Several persons besides Peronneau were asked to give their estimates of the value of the office which Peronneau had lost to the revolutionary government. Their estimates ranged between £1,500 and £2,000 sterling (£10,500 and £14,000 South Carolina currency) per year; the commissions were only about £800 sterling (£5,600 currency) of that amount. The estimates probably were on the high side—it would have been to Peronneau's advantage to overrate the value of the office—but it is apparent that the commissions were the smaller part of the public treasurer's income. From whatever source, the public treasurer was well compensated. John Hopton testified that the "Office of Treasurer was considered as a very lucrative Office—Superior in Emolument to the Governor."[75]

Eighteenth-century political morality saw nothing wrong with such intermingling of public and private funds to the financial benefit of the office holder, as long as the custodian of the public funds could produce them whenever they were needed by the public. Indeed, that morality seems to have seen nothing especially reprehensible about the official's getting considerably in arrears. Jacob Motte was found to have a serious deficit in 1752, but he was not removed from office, and when he died in 1770 it was discovered that once more he owed very large sums to the Treasury.

CONSEQUENCES OF INTERMINGLED FUNDS

The deficiency of 1752 was brought to light by the hurricane which struck Charles Town on September 15, 1752. A few weeks later Motte presented a memorial to the Commons House stating that the hurricane and "some other unfortunate Incidents which happened before" had so impoverished him that he thought it imperative that his public accounts be examined and settled. Indicating that his assets probably would not cover the amount of public moneys entrusted to him, he asked for reasonable time to pay any balance that might be due. Immediately both houses of the Assembly assigned members to take the memorial into consideration.[76]

Governor Glen expressed his alarm over the situation and communicated the news that Motte had refused to redeem the certificates of indebtedness that he had issued to public creditors in anticipation of tax collections. Glen was afraid that the public credit would suffer a tremendous blow (the certificates were a legal liability of the province), and he said that he proposed "some thing" to the Council to keep the certificates from becoming worthless. Despite the seriousness of the situation, the Commons House was unwilling to act. It was near the end of the Assembly's usual time of sitting and many members had already gone home. The Commons House asked for, and eventually got, an adjournment until late November.[77]

What Glen proposed to the Council is uncertain; the journals do not record any suggestions. Just after the adjournment of the Assembly, however, the Council decided that Motte should be required to deliver to itself and Governor Glen all the bonds and notes in his possession. Accordingly, he turned over a sum of £36,182 3s 1d.[78]

Nothing else was done before the reconvening of the Assembly six weeks later. At that time the Commons House resolved that the security for Motte's bond was liable for the redemption of the tax certificates and that the Commons House itself would make up any deficiency so that holders of the certificates would suffer no loss. (Motte's security was Gabriel Manigault, the former public treasurer, who was bound in the sum of £7,000 sterling or about £49,000 South Carolina currency. It must have been sobering to him to hear the Commons House imply that the entire sum of the bond might be spent without extinguishing the debt.) In order to secure further the debt due from Motte to the public, it was decided that Motte should mortgage his property. The Commons House ordered Motte to deposit all the moneys in his hands with Manigault, who was to be solely responsible for their handling until the Assembly determined otherwise. In effect, Manigault was to be acting public treasurer until the accounts were settled. But he refused to accept the position, and the money was eventually placed with Chief Justice Charles Pinckney and Speaker James Michie.[79]

A report of an investigating committee showed that there was

a balance due from the duty funds of £20,955 5s, and that
£27,372 in moneys of various sorts was in Motte's hands. Of this
amount, the committee sealed up £25,722 and left £1,650 un-
sealed to meet current demands on the Treasury. Motte therefore
had more than enough cash on hand to account for the duty
funds entrusted to him. In addition, he presented a list of £7,149
1s 8d due him from merchants for duties, which probably would
be collected soon. The grave financial condition was caused by the
large numbers of certificates of indebtedness which were still in
circulation and which, if presented for redemption, could bank-
rupt the Treasury. The committee was unable to ascertain the
amount of tax certificates outstanding, but it estimated that there
might be £70,000.[80] Motte turned in to the Council an inventory
of his estate, showing a worth of £27,426 18s.[81] The mortgages
were completed by the end of December, but it was 1759 before
all the work of the trustees was finally completed.[82]

The experience of being liable for a bond of £7,000 sterling
was enough to unsettle the nerves of even so wealthy a man as
Gabriel Manigault. He intimated to Motte that the amount was
too great for a single person to carry, and Motte presented a
memorial to the Commons House setting forth Manigault's desire
to be relieved of some of the burden and the willingness of others
to become sureties. Twenty-five persons, mostly merchants and
professional men, agreed to join Manigault, which made each
liable for only £270 sterling, or about £1,890 South Carolina currency.[83] Acting with the apparent motive of forming a "pool" to
insure that no one person would be financially ruined by his
obligation as a surety for a public official, there may have been the
motive of shielding Motte from the consequences of what they
regarded as an unavoidable disaster. And the sureties were naturally interested in seeing that public credit did not collapse.

It was by no means certain that Motte had permanently dam-
aged the public credit, however. In normal times outstanding tax
certificates frequently represented a sum greater than the cash on
hand in the Treasury. As long as there was no run on the Treasury, there was no cause for alarm. By the time the certificates
were presented for redemption, there would probably be enough
cash on hand. Something like this seems to have happened. The

journals are very sketchy, but it appears that the accounts were untangled without undue difficulty. Matters had progressed by early March 1753 to the point that the Commons House ordered the sealed moneys put back into circulation.[84]

The crisis was ended. Throughout the affair there was not the slightest hint that anyone blamed Motte for what had happened. He remained in office, continuing to serve as public treasurer until his death in 1770. But Motte apparently learned little from his near disaster of 1752. He lost £28,000 in 1767 in the bankruptcy of the firm of Middleton, Liston, & Hope because he had allowed the firm that much credit in paying its import duties.[85] And at the time of his death, there was a deficiency in the Treasury of £124,734 8s 5d, for which his estate was held liable.[86]

AN IMPERFECT MECHANISM

Motte's irregularities point up a great divergence between theory and practice in the Public Treasury. In fact, the conduct of at least four of the ten public treasurers[87] ran counter to the Assembly's intention that the public treasurer should serve as custodian of funds whose disposal was entirely at the discretion of the Assembly, not that of the official. The public treasurer, however, often regarded the funds as his own capital and used them for private profit. It is ironic that the processes of government came more than once to a standstill as the two houses of the legislature quarreled over the right to spend a few hundred pounds, while Alexander Parris and Jacob Motte plundered the Treasury for tens of thousands of pounds, and Henry Peronneau and Benjamin Dart so tied up funds that the Treasury was "kept in a state of Beggary and want...."[88]

Such seems to have been the nature of eighteenth-century politics. When one considers the difficulties of establishing a fiscal system under conditions that made success seem unlikely, one is inclined to remember Dr. Samuel Johnson's remark about dogs walking and women preaching: "It is not done well; but you are surprised to find it done at all." The Public Treasury worked badly some of the time, but, surprisingly, the system, despite its numerous shortcomings, did work. However imperfectly, it met a need.

NOTES

[1]*The Statutes-at-Large of South Carolina,* ed. Thomas Cooper and David McCord (10 vols.; Columbia, 1836–1841), II, 64–65.

[2]Copies of his accounts were sometimes sent to the Board of Trade, however. See, for example, C.O. 5/512.

[3]Edson L. Whitney, *Government of the Colony of South Carolina* (Baltimore, 1895), 45–46.

[4]The original act is not extant, but the bond is referred to in Commons House Journal, November 4, 1700, *Journal of the Commons House of Assembly of South Carolina for the Session Beginning October 30, 1700, and Ending November 16, 1700,* ed. A.S. Salley (Columbia, 1924), 10, and in an act of 1703, *Statutes,* II, 205.

[5]See Chapter VI.

[6]*Statutes,* II, 204, 306, 351; III, 148; IV, 326–27; Commons House Journal, March 28, 1735, *Journal of the Commons House of Assembly of South Carolina, November 8, 1734–June 7, 1735,* ed. A.S. Salley (Columbia, 1947), 154–55.

[7]Upper House Journal, March 29, 1735, CJ, VI, Part One, 89.

[8]The forms of these oaths may be found in Commons House Journal, March 7, 1705/6, *Journal of the Commons House of Assembly of South Carolina, March 6, 1705/6 –April 9, 1706,* ed. A.S. Salley (Columbia, 1937), 6–8.

[9]*Statutes,* III, 201. The oath was almost identical with the one prescribed during the proprietary period. Ibid., II, 657. The difference in wording is slight and probably of no significance. In addition to this oath, the public treasurer had to take a separate oath to comply with the provision of the Jury Act. Ibid., III, 282.

[10]Ibid., III, 201–2.

[11]Ibid., IV, 326.

[12]Commons House Journal, June 23, 1748, *The Colonial Records of South Carolina: The Journal of the Commons House of Assembly, January 19, 1748–June 29, 1748,* ed. J.H. Easterby and Ruth S. Green (Columbia, 1961), 349.

[13]All are deposited in the South Carolina Department of Archives and History, Columbia, S.C. At one time another ledger covering the years 1740 to 1747 was included with the records of the public treasurer, but it obviously was a private ledger, and Miss Wylma Wates has identified it as belonging to John Royer, nephew of Gabriel Manigault, one of the public treasurers. It is my belief that Royer handled Manigault's private business while Manigault was public treasurer, and that association may explain the journal's being included in the Treasury group by early archivists. Maurice A. Crouse, "Gabriel Manigault: Charleston Merchant," *South Carolina Historical Magazine,* LXVIII (1967), 222.

[14]Parris was seriously deficient at times, especially in reissuing public orders which should have been canceled (see Chapter II), but he was not as bad as M. Eugene Sirmans makes him out to be in *Colonial South Carolina: A Political History, 1663–1763* (Chapel Hill, 1966), 165–66. Sirmans' charge that Parris owed £40,000 to the Treasury and could not pay it back is based on a misreading of the Treasury records and of the appropriations act of 1731. If Sirmans' interpretation is correct, Parris reduced his "debt" from £38,359 18s 7½d to £9,157 7s 6½d between Sep-

tember 29, 1728, and January 4, 1728/9, merely by disbursing much more than the fund received in income from duties. Ledger, 1725–1730, 122, 137. This, of course, was impossible. The several "Ballance[s] due to the Public" are obviously bookkeeping statements of the cash on hand: the sums are always carried to the next cash account as credits, are added to the income from duties during the accounting period, and are offset by expenditures from the fund. When the appropriations act stated that there was £40,000 unapplied in the Treasury, it was not "to protect Parris's reputation"; the money was really there, ready to be applied to payment of public debts. Ibid., 69, 99, 122, 137; *Statutes*, III, 334–41.

[15]Although sometimes cited as "Ledger A" because it is the earliest surviving record, it contains references to balances carried to a new "Ledger D." Ledger 1725–1730, 93, 99, 126, 137. There certainly should be a ledger to fill the gap between 1730 and 1735, and it is plausible that Parris would have filled two ledgers ("A" and "B") from 1712 to 1725.

[16]Council Journal, July 2, 1744, XI, Part Two, 374. It is not clear whether they were destroyed before or after Manigault took office succeeding Parris, nor is it clear who destroyed them or why. In light of Parris' difficulties, it is not inconceivable that he destroyed them himself.

[17]Ledger B, 48, 75.

[18]Folio 10 of Ledger B listed a balance of £10,970 4s 7¼d, which was carried forward to folio 13 as £10,970 4s 6¾d.

[19]Publick's Ledger, 1771–1776, 13–14; Upper House Journal, August 11, 1773, C.O. 5/478, 6.

[20]Ledger B, 57, 61, 76, 80; John Savage to William Henry Lyttelton, November 8, 13, 15, 1759, Lyttelton Papers, William L. Clement Library.

[21]Ledger B, 41, 43.

[22]Commons House Journal, March 8, 1737/8, *The Colonial Records of South Carolina: The Journal of the Commons House of Assembly, November 10, 1736–June 7, 1739,* ed. J.H. Easterby (Columbia, 1951), 526.

[23]Commons House Journal, March 8, 1737/8, February 23, 1738/9, ibid., 527, 644–45.

[24]Commons House Journal, May 7, 1743, *The Colonial Records of South Carolina: The Journal of the Commons House of Assembly, September 14, 1742–January 27, 1744,* ed. J.H. Easterby (Columbia, 1954), 455.

[25]Commons House Journal, April 11, 1744, *The Colonial Records of South Carolina: The Journal of the Commons House of Assembly, February 20, 1744–May 25, 1745,* ed. J.H. Easterby (Columbia, 1955), 83.

[26]Ledger B, 54.

[27]See Chapters II and IV for descriptions of the procedure involved.

[28]Commons House Journal, February 25, 1740/1, *The Colonial Records of South Carolina: The Journal of the Commons House of Assembly, September 12, 1739–March 26, 1741,* ed. J.H. Easterby (Columbia, 1952), 507.

[29]See Chapter VI.

[30]Council Journal, February 25,1742/3, X, 17.

[31]See Chapter VI for a discussion of the controversy of 1737 over new township funds.

[32]Commons House Journal, June 1, 1738, *JCH, 1736–1739,* 572.

[33]"Account of Cash Disboursed by Gabriel Manigault Publick Treasurer for the use of the Province from the 25th March 1740 to the 29th January Following . . . ," Manigault Family Papers, South Carolina Historical Society.

[34]Commons House Journal, January 22, 1741/2, *The Colonial Records of South Carolina: The Journal of the Commons House of Assembly, May 18, 1741–July 10, 1742*, ed. J.H. Easterby (Columbia, 1953), 329–30.

[35]*Statutes*, II, 64. Apparently there was no deputy during the period 1710–1717. Ibid., III, 1.

[36]Ibid., III, 1–2.

[37]Commons House Journal, August 23, 1770, XXXVIII, Part Two, 423.

[38]*Statutes*, II, 202. Before 1703 the functions of the office were performed by the secretary of the province or various magistrates. Ibid., 64–65, 111.

[39]Ibid., 202.

[40]Ibid., III, 413; Commons House Journal, May 11, 1736, IX, Part Two, 667–68. The efficiency of the deputies is questionable. There was constant turnover in personnel, and records of collections received from them are rare.

[41]*Statutes*, II, 652, 654–55; III, 61–62.

[42]See Chapter IV for a full discussion of taxation procedure.

[43]Jack P. Greene, *The Quest for Power: The Lower Houses of Assembly in the Southern Royal Colonies, 1689–1776* (Chapel Hill, 1963), 459.

[44]*Calendar of State Papers, Colonial Series, America and West Indies, 1574——*, ed. W. Noel Sainsbury, et al. (44 vols. to 1969; London, 1860——), XV, 390; XVI. 112.

[45]See Greene, *Quest for Power*, 245–48.

[46]*Statutes*, III, 148. During the proprietary period, before this act was passed, several public receivers continued as members of the Commons House during their terms.

[47]James Glen to Duke of Bedford, October 10, 1748, Records in the British Public Record Office Relating to South Carolina, 1663–1782, comp. W. Noel Sainsbury (36 manuscript vols.), XXIII, 234–35. These records, copied from originals in the B.P.R.O., are in the S.C. Dept. of Archives and History.

[48]See, for example, the notes about arms and ammunition in Commons House Journal, August 28, 1701, *Journal of the Commons House of Assembly of South Carolina for the Session Beginning August 13, 1701, and Ending August 28, 1701*, ed. A.S. Salley (Columbia, 1926), 28–29; August 25, 1702, *Journal of the Commons House of Assembly of South Carolina for 1702*, ed. A.S. Salley (Columbia, 1932), 72–73.

[49]*Statutes*, III, 181. It may be that this authorization constituted the appointment instead of there being a specific ordinance.

[50]Ibid., 187.

[51]For a discussion of these townships, see Robert L. Meriwether, *The Expansion of South Carolina* (Kingsport, Tenn., 1940), 17–30.

[52]Commons House Journal, March 6, 1734/5, March 25, 28, 1735, *JCH, 1734–1735*, 96–97, 123, 134, 154.

[53]*Statutes*, III, 279. The grand jury list contained the names of persons who paid more than £5 in taxes; petit jurors were those who paid 20s; and special jurors were the taxpayers of Charles Town proper. W. Roy Smith, *South Carolina as a Royal Province* (New York, 1903), 126–27.

[54]*South-Carolina Gazette*, May 24, 1735; May 1, 1736; April 9, 1737.

[55]It is possible, however, that no serious attempt was made to collect these fees. They are mentioned very seldom in the Treasury records.

[56]*Statutes*, III, 715–18. The statute does not mention the role of the public treasurer, but one section was not printed by the editors. For a typical advertisement, see *South-Carolina Gazette and Country Journal*, March 11, 1766.

[57]*Statutes*, III, 413.

[58]Commons House Journal, February 7, 1736/7, *JCH, 1736–1739*, 219.

[59]*Statutes*, II, 66.

[60]Commons House Journal, April 6, 1706, *JCH, 1706*, 52.

[61]*Statutes*, II, 306.

[62]Ibid., III, 1.

[63]Ibid., 68. Although the fortifications duty act did not mention commissions at all, Gabriel Manigault, in his first full accounts submitted in March 1737/8, included commissions on receiving and paying out of that fund. He argued by analogy with other funds that commissions should be allowed, and the Assembly agreed. Commons House Journal, March 8, 1737/8, *JCH, 1736–1739*, 522. Rejection of this claim would have reduced the Public Treasurer's income substantially, for the fortifications fund was at the time one of the more active funds.

[64]*Statutes*, III, 567.

[65]Ibid., 422. The fee structure was changed from time to time but does not seem to have affected the public treasurer materially.

[66]But Robert Peronneau, testifying after the Revolution on behalf of his brother Henry, said that Henry derived £400 sterling from such fees annually, "Historical Notes," *South Carolina Historical and Genealogical Magazine*, XIII (1912), 229.

[67]Ledger B, 2, 10, 13, 16, 19, 23, 25, 28, 32, 37, 48, 51, 57, 61–62, 67, 72, 75–76, 80, 83; Publick's Ledger, 1771–1776, 13–14.

[68]Upper House Journal, May 24, 1744, CJ, XII, 74.

[69]*Commons House Journal*, March 1, 5, 1736/7, *JCH, 1736–1739*, 262, 326.

[70]Commons House Journal, January 16, March 21, 1744/5, *JCH, 1744–1745*, 276, 404. Jacob Motte was sometimes paid small sums for making out tax-indebtedness certificates. Commons House Journal, June 11, 1747, *The Colonial Records of South Carolina: The Journal of the Commons House of Assembly, September 10, 1746–June 13, 1747*, ed. J.H. Easterby and Ruth S. Green (Columbia, 1958), 360, 372; *June 23, 1748, JCH, 1748*, 348–49.

[71]Commons House Journal, May 16–17, 1744, *JCH, 1744–1745*, 145–49, 155–57.

[72]Upper House Journal, May 24, 1744, CJ, XII, 70–74. The curtain line was part of the fortifications of Charles Town.

[73]Upper House Journal, May 24, 1745, CJ, XIII, 249–50.

[74]Upper House Journal, August 24, 1773, C.O. 5/478, 14; Commons House Journal, September 10, 1773, XXXIX, 2d pagination, 91.

[75]Transcripts of the Manuscript books and Papers of the Commission of inquiry into Losses and Services of the American Loyalists held under Acts 23, 25, 26, 28 and 29 of George III preserved amongst the Audit Office Records of the Public Record Office of England, 1783–1790 (60 volumes transcribed for the New York Public Library, 1898–1903), LII, 505–32.

[76]Commons House Journal, October 5–6, 1752, XXVII, Part Two, 609–10, 625.

[77]Commons House Journal, October 7, 1752, ibid., 641–44, 647.

[78]Council Journal, October 7, 1752, XX, Part Two, 422–25.

[79]Commons House Journal, November 24–25, 1752, XXVIII, Part One, 14–16, 33–34, 37.

[80]Commons House Journal, December 7, 1752, ibid., 95–96. Tax certificates might pass current for years before being redeemed. There might therefore be considerable amounts of them outstanding at any given time.

[81]Upper House Journal, December 6, 1752, CJ, XIX, 2d pagination, 122.

[82]Records of the Mesne Conveyance Office, Charleston, S.C., N N, 70–86; Commons House Journal, April 7, 1759, XXXII, 2d pagination, 225–26.

[83]Commons House Journal, March 1–2, April 18, 1753, XXVIII, Part One, 275, 288–89, 521; Miscellaneous Records, I I (or J J), 678–703, S.C. Dept. of Archives and History.

[84]Commons House Journal, March 5, 1753, XXXVIII, Part One, 318.

[85]Henry Laurens to William Reeve, October 2, 1767, "Correspondence of Henry Laurens," ed. Joseph W. Barnwell, *South Carolina Historical and Genealogical Magazine*, XXVIII (1927), 213.

[86]Council Journal, February 25, 1771, XXXVI, Part One, 55.

[87]The charges of short entries made against Thomas Smith may have been politically inspired. Commons House Journal, April 24, 1703, *Journal of the Commons House of Assembly of South Carolina for 1703*, ed. A.S. Salley (Columbia, 1934), 68. But they may have been perfectly well founded, in which case Smith would join the list of public servants whose services were not always in the public interest.

[88]Upper House Journal, August 24, 1773, C.O. 5/478, 13–14.

CHAPTER II

The Problem of the Currency

B Y THE TIME that royal government was established in South
Carolina in 1721, the question of the currency had already
caused considerable agitation and distress. For the next ten years
it would cause even more. A major issue, it led to sharply divided
factions within the province and to virtual civil war and a complete breakdown of the Assembly. But with the general settlement
of public affairs under Governor Robert Johnson in 1731 the
problem of the currency was "solved" about as well as it would
ever be.

COINAGE

The difficulty lay in a problem common to all the colonies—the
lack of an adequate circulating medium of exchange. South
Carolinians were no luckier than their neighbors in being able to
hold on to gold and silver, whether of English or foreign coinage.
Substantial sums of coin seem to have entered the province,
chiefly from the West Indies. The report on currency made in
1740 mentions Spanish pieces of eight, double "Ryals," "Ryals,"
"Lyon Dollars," English crowns, "Rix Dollars," French crowns,
pistoles, Louis d'ors, "Arabian gold," and English guineas,[1] and
the Treasury had in 1771 some £59,520 5s to £61,269 2s 3d in
Spanish, Portuguese, and English coins, in seventeen varieties or
denominations.[2] But the pieces were in short supply among the
people, being used mostly to settle accounts with English merchants who were leery of colonial paper and demanded cash or

good bills of exchange. South Carolina tried overvaluing foreign coins to attract them to the province and perhaps keep them there. In the years around 1700, the valuation of Spanish coins was such that lightweight pieces of eight were being accepted at 61 percent more than their intrinsic value. Despite Queen Anne's Proclamation of 1704 and parliamentary legislation of 1708, which attempted to limit overvaluation to no more than 33⅓ percent, South Carolina for some time held to its former level.[3] After the large issues of paper currency, the province seems to have depended less on overvaluation of foreign coins. In 1752 the public treasurer was authorized to receive Spanish dollars at £1 11s 10d, which, allowing for the seven-to-one ratio which then existed between currency and sterling, was about ½d above the legal rate of 4s 6d.[4] Early in 1771 there was a voluntary agreement among the citizens of Charles Town to receive foreign coins at higher rates than formerly. The value of the Spanish dollar was placed at slightly less than 4s 8d sterling, hardly a drastic overvaluation. Still, it was enough to create a profit of £1,749 0s 3d for the Public Treasury on its holdings of foreign coins and to "set Abundance of Gold & Silver at Liberty, which has been a long Time locked up."[5]

Besides overvaluation of foreign coins, the province sought other means of adding to the supply of coins. In 1746 the Commons House debated as to how "Woods money" might be added to the currency. From the description given, the pieces must have been the copper coinage issued by William Wood in the early 1720s intended for circulation in the American colonies. The coins were issued in denominations of 2d, 1d, and ½d and bore the design of a rose and the slogan *Rosa Americana Utile Dulci* ("American rose, the useful with the pleasant"). A committee reported that Gabriel Manigault had 2,083 pounds of the coins in all three denominations and proposed that the coins be valued at 6d, 4d, and 3d, respectively, which would have added £287 to the currency in the form of small change. The Commons House, however, rejected the proposal, as it did two other proposals to value Wood's coinage more highly. There seems to have been no resolution of the matter, but the coins may have circulated anyway for what they would bring in the marketplace.[6]

In 1771 the joint public treasurers Henry Peronneau and Benjamin Dart commissioned Henry Laurens to secure in England a small issue of £100 sterling in coins or tokens to serve as small change. Laurens encountered nothing but frustration in trying to fulfill the request. He was first assured that there would be little delay, but the mint had none of the ½d coins desired. Laurens then found that an order from the board of the Treasury would be necessary, and he was told that it did not readily grant orders for such small sums. On the other hand, others who had had dealings with the Treasury said that it would not issue above £40 sterling. Finally, in April 1772, Laurens was able to report that £108 sterling value in ½d coins would be ready and shipped within the week. Since standard references on early American coinage do not record anything about a distinctive issue, it is presumed that the coins were regular British issues, but Laurens had noted in his last letter on the subject that he had once thought of having tokens stamped in Birmingham with a "a Device proper for our Latitude," consisting of the figure of either Britannia or America on one side and a sheaf of rice on the other.[7] Whatever their design, they no doubt were eagerly accepted by a currency-starved province.

BILLS OF CREDIT

Various courses were open to a colony which lacked sufficient currency. Perhaps the most obvious, but not necessarily the best, solution was to resort to barter. The province used this method at least as early as 1687, when an act provided that commodities such as corn, Indian and English peas, pork, beef, tobacco, and tar could be used to pay debts at established prices unless the payment agreement specifically called for gold, silver, or a particular commodity. The "rice bills" of 1719 and 1720, although a form of paper money, were to be redeemed by payment of taxes in rice at certain predetermined prices.[8]

But after Massachusetts demonstrated in 1690 that a paper money issue could work, at least after a fashion, the natural but dangerous solution to currency problems was the issuing of "square money."[9] South Carolina was the second North American colony to issue paper money, doing so in 1703 to finance an expedition against the Spaniards at St. Augustine in one of the episodes of Queen Anne's War. Bills bearing interest at 12 percent were issued in the amount of £6,000 and were to be redeemed by various taxes and duties within the next two years.[10] But the bills had hardly been issued when the Assembly found reasons to postpone redemption and divert the sinking fund to payment of more pressing current debts. Apparently none had been redeemed by July 5, 1707, when the Assembly voted to issue £8,000 to cover the costs of building a fort at Charles Town. The Assembly added £3,000 on February 14, 1707/8, £5,000 on April 24, 1708, £3,000 on March 1, 1710/11, and £4,000 on November 10, 1711. Only the latter issue (called "Tuscarora bills" because they were issued to help fight the war against the Tuscarora Indians in North Carolina) had any provision for redemption by a special fund.[11] Together, the various acts for issuing bills of credit present a terribly confusing jumble of figures, for each act, except the one which authorized the Tuscarora bills, replaced at least part of a previous issue with newly printed bills; the amount in circulation was therefore less than the sum of all the issues. The 1740 account of the currency bears evidence of a certain amount of guesswork on the part of its author—all figures are in exact thousands; some £6,000 are written off as sunk, lost, or destroyed, with no indication of relative proportions—but in the absence of other evidence, it may be accepted as an explanation of the status of the currency in 1712 when a new plan was devised. The account estimates that in 1712 there remained in circulation £16,000 of the unsecured bills of credit and the entire Tuscarora issue of £4,000, for a total of £20,000.[12]

By what was known as the Bank Act, the Assembly on June 7, 1712, called in all previous issues except the Tuscarora bills and reprinted them. It added £4,000 in bills of credit which were apparently unsecured, but the main feature of the act was the issuing of £32,000 to be lent to individuals on the principle of the land bank, the first time such a bank was used in the English colonies. The concept of the land bank was simple enough. The currency problem was caused more by the lack of an adequate circulating medium of exchange than by a lack of wealth itself. Property of any sort, and especially land and slaves, obviously had some value but could not be used conveniently as a medium of exchange. The problem was one of translating the values of land and slaves into money values. The land bank offered a scheme by which this could be done: planters could retain full use of their property and still create a money supply by mortgaging their property to the land bank. The Bank Act provided that any person could borrow between £100 and £300 from the bank at 12½ percent interest per year for a twelve-year period, provided only that he give as security a mortgage on land or slaves worth twice the amount of the loan. The notes issued by the bank would be legal tender for all debts, so they would make a positive addition to the currency supply of the province. The planter would retain full use of the property and would receive all profits from that use, out of which he would be expected to repay the principal and interest on the loan. If he made all payments on schedule, he would regain title to his pledged security, and in the meantime he and the entire province would have benefited from the circulation of the notes which made buying and selling possible on a money basis rather than by barter.[13]

Such was the theory of the bank. It is difficult to judge how well it worked for South Carolina. Apparently the issues were made without difficulty; in 1723 some £8,000 of the Bank Act bills were said to still be in circulation. But whatever success the Bank Act may have had was overridden by the large new issues of bills of credit in the next few years, which led to serious depreciation of all bills. The Assembly issued £50,000 in unsecured bills of credit within the interval of less than a year during the war against the Yamassee Indians in 1715 and 1716.[14] Although the Assembly went through the motions of providing for the redemption of the issues, redemption was postponed several times and rice was made a commodity for redemption of a part of the bills. To add to the chaos, the Assembly in 1719 and 1720 made two issues of new "rice bills" totaling £34,000 and in 1723 added £40,000 more to the bills of credit in addition to reprinting all the old issues. The total outstanding at that time was estimated to be £120,000.[15]

The act of February 23, 1722/3, had been passed only after

strenuous objection by the Council, and on August 27, 1723, it was declared repealed by the authorities in England along with part of an earlier act which had reissued some of the rice bills.[16] Bowing to the Board of Trade's injunction to Governor Francis Nicholson that the affected issues must be retired, the Assembly on February 15, 1723/4, specified that notes of the new issue of £40,000 and the £15,000 in rice bills could be used solely for the payment of taxes or provincial duties and would be canceled when so received. The act left a considerable amount of currency not subject to redemption, and only about £13,500 of the earmarked notes were actually redeemed.[17]

On two points paper-money advocates in the Assembly fought bitterly with the Council and its president, Arthur Middleton (who became the chief executive after Nicholson's return to England in 1725). First, they wanted to prevent the redemption of existing issues of paper money by diverting the sinking funds to other purposes, such as defense. Second, they wanted to make positive additions to the currency supply by issuing even more paper money, arguing that the supply was not sufficient.[18] Despite furious battles in the Assembly and a virtual state of civil war in the province, the only concession that Middleton and the Council would make was to divert sinking fund recipts to an expedition against St. Augustine in 1727.[19] And the province never again was allowed to issue new bills of credit, although other expedients were devised which accomplished much the same purpose.

The currency question eventually became fairly well stabilized by an act of August 20, 1731, passed as part of the general settlement of problems that had plagued the province during Middleton's administration. Because £13,500 had actually been redeemed under the terms of the act of February 15, 1723/4, there remained only £106,500 in circulation. All old bills were called in, to be replaced by a new printing which was not subject to redemption at all. This issue was, until the American Revolution, a substantial part of the currency supply, but not all of it, as partisans of paper money sometimes argued. Because of the severe depreciation of the bills during the early 1720s, the South Carolina currency was worth only about one-seventh its value in sterling terms.

The ratio of seven-to-one prevailed generally throughout the rest of the colonial period.[20]

The Assembly tried in 1736 and again in 1746 to secure approval of an addition to the currency. The plan of 1736 would have reprinted the old issues (estimated at only £100,000 in this case) and would have issued £110,000 more in new bills on the same principle as the Bank Act of 1712. The act provided for eventually placing all currency upon the bank principle.[21] In defense of the new issue the Commons House argued that the mere issuing of bills of credit did not cause inflation of prices. South Carolina's difficulties with currency values they attributed to adverse balances of trade, the general rise in volume of trade, and particularly the large importations of slaves (nearly £840,000 worth had been imported within the previous two years). They emphasized the scarcity of currency by asserting that three or four planters, merely by selling their crops, had been able to get into their hands practically all the currency of the province, so that merchants were forced to buy country produce on credit. John Locke was quoted to the effect that "Money is necessary to the carrying on of Trade, and where that fails Trade must stop";[22] but all to no avail. The act had a suspending clause which prevented its operation until the king's assent was given, and the king did not approve. The attempt of 1746 began and ended almost identically.[23]

The paper bills quickly became worn, dirty, and torn, so there were frequent acts of the Assembly to exchange and reprint them. Besides the reprintings already noted, there were general reprintings of the entire currency in 1748 and 1769.[24] In addition, there were limited reprintings of £20,000 in 1752 and 1761.[25] There may well have been other reprintings which were authorized by clauses of acts dealing primarily with other subjects. An act of 1735 on counterfeiting, for example, called for reprinting £10,000 to replace old bills.[26]

PUBLIC ORDERS

Along with the reprinting of the bills of credit in 1731 another device was used for adding, at least temporarily, to the money supply of the province—the public order. Because of the controversies in the Assembly, there had been no tax bill passed since 1727. The debt of the province in 1731 stood at £104,775 1s 3¼d. Because no previous tax had ever raised more than £35,000 in a single year, it was manifestly impossible that the debt could be extinguished by a single year's taxation. On the same day that Governor Johnson approved the act for reprinting the bills of credit, he also assented to an act creating public orders for £104,775 1s 3¼d to pay off old debts. In most respects, public orders can hardly be distinguished from bills of credit, but there is one important distinction: they were receivable only for the payment of taxes or import and export duties. (Although not a legal tender for private debts, they doubtless circulated among individuals because of their guaranteed acceptance at the Treasury.) The orders of 1731 were to be issued in denominations from £5 to £50 and were to bear interest at 5 percent per year until paid (no later issue of public orders seems to have carried interest). The issue was tied to the Negro duty fund, the receipts from the duty on slaves imported into the province. The interest would be paid from that fund; up to £8,500 annually for the next seven years would be taken from the fund to cancel the orders received by the public treasurer; and the orders could be used in payment of the Negro duty (or any other duty, for that matter). In effect, the public orders anticipated the collecting of £8,500 annually from the import duty. The public treasurer was placed under a strict obligation to account for the orders by number and not to reissue them but actually to cancel them.[27] As W. Roy Smith remarks, it is difficult to see how the orders could have been redeemed within seven years, although an additional sum of £40,000 already accumulated in the Negro duty fund was also to be applied toward redemption. The total amount at the end of that time would have been at best (assuming cancellation of the maximum amount annually) only £99,500, not the full £104,775 1s 3¼d.[28]

This, South Carolina's first issue of public orders, could not be termed an unqualified success. In January 1734/5 the Council appears to have become concerned that the orders were not being canceled properly and fearful of the possible repercussions in England. The Commons House appointed a committee to investigate the accounts.[29] The committee uncovered enough information to warrant a full-scale investigation into Parris's conduct of office, and in March a new committee returned a serious indictment. Andrew Rutledge, the chairman, charged that over a period of nearly four years Parris had reissued a total of £32,780 in public orders instead of canceling them as required by law. Furthermore, Parris had kept no record of those reissued nor of the interest allowed on them until two weeks prior to the report, since which time only £633 13s had been recorded and could be identified. Further accusations made it clear why Parris had neglected to keep records. According to the law, interest on the orders was to be allowed only when they were presented in payment of duties. Rutledge said that Parris had paid interest to their holders even when the orders had not been used to pay duties. Also, it appears that, as a favor to importers, he had even allowed interest on the ordinary promissory notes given by them in payment of duties instead of orders, interest for which there was no legal basis whatever. Immediately upon considering the evidence, the Commons House censured Parris and took steps to remove him from office.[30]

Despite the urgency of the situation, the Assembly moved very slowly in settling Parris's accounts. The records give few details, but it appears that Parris and the new public treasurer, Gabriel Manigault, were expected to jointly work out an adjustment. The Assembly leniently decided that, as a matter of common justice, Parris should be allowed to endorse the interest on public orders received into the Treasury until he had endorsed the amount that he had illegally allowed.[31] Parris turned over to Manigault and to the Assembly all the orders, notes, and bonds in his possession and offered to mortgage his real and personal estate to secure the amount due to the public.[32] It took nearly three years of investigating and calculating before even a preliminary settlement of the accounts was made. According to calculations, Parris's estate (for he had died in 1736) was liable for £54,789 14s 5¾d. This sum was reduced by various allowances and adjustments, and in March 1737/8 the Commons House announced that the estate owed £27,171 4s 5¼d, for which it asked that security be given.[33] The mortgaged properties, including half of an island on Port

Royal River (still known as Parris Island), were not easy to sell, and one lot in Beaufort remained unsold in January 1752, when it was estimated that its sale would finally bring in enough money to pay off Parris' debt completely.[34]

Understandably, the Assembly proceeded cautiously with its next issue of public orders and might not have resorted to them at all if the defense of Georgia and South Carolina against Spanish attack had not made public orders necessary in 1737. An issue of £35,010 was to be printed, from which the commissioners of fortifications could draw to build a "curtain line" to prevent naval attack upon Charles Town, as could the commanders of two warships defending Georgia to pay their expenses. The orders would pass current for five years for the payment of any tax or duty except the Negro duty (because that duty was already being used to redeem the 1731 issue), and would be retired by five years of taxation and receipts from the fortifications duty. To assure that there would be no reissuing of the orders, the canceled orders were to be burned to ashes annually in the presence of a joint committee of the two houses of the Assembly.[35]

The letter of the law was not strictly followed, but this time it was the Assembly rather than the public treasurer that violated it. In September 1738 the Commons House resolved to let the commissioners of fortifications draw upon £3,000 which had been designated for sinking the orders.[36] As a result of this and possible other similar actions the orders were not entirely redeemed within five years. In fact, in November 1742, when they all should have been redeemed, it was reported that only £19,920 10s 11¼d had been burned. As late as March 1754 there were still a few outstanding.[37]

The experience with the 1737 issue was encouraging enough, however, inasmuch as the province used the scheme of public orders four times within the next few years to provide £119,508 for defense purposes. In April 1740 the Assembly authorized an issue of £25,000 along with a loan from General James Oglethorpe for £2,000 sterling at 8 percent interest, the total to be South Carolina's contribution toward Oglethorpe's expedition against St. Augustine. Both the loan and public orders were to be paid off by special taxes through 1744.[38] By September the plans had changed. Instead of getting a loan from Oglethorpe, the Assembly had decided to borrow £15,000 currency (roughly £2,000 sterling) from Treasury funds and to issue new public orders for £11,508 to be redeemed by a special tax in 1745.[39] Again in 1742, when the Spaniards were attacking Georgia and threatening South Carolina, the Assembly authorized an issue of public orders for defense. The sum of £63,000 was to be redeemed by an annual tax for the next ten years.[40] In May 1745, the Assembly authorized the commissioners of fortifications to issue orders amounting to £20,000 to pay for land acquisitions and construction costs. These were to be accepted in payment of the fortification duty and retired from that fund.[41] In May 1755 a similar act was passed allowing the public treasurer to issue orders for £33,600 for general defense, which were to be accepted for all taxes and to be retired by four years of taxation.[42]

The largest issues of public orders came as a result of the French and Indian War. In July 1757 the Assembly authorized three separate issues of public orders totaling £229,300 to cover the expenses of fortifying Charles Town, repairing Fort Johnson, and maintaining Colonel Probarth Howarth's regiment for a year. This amount was to be redeemed by taxation for the next five years and an additional duty on imported goods.[43] There were two issues in 1760 for campaigns against the Cherokee Indians. In July the Assembly authorized £316,693 2s 5d to be redeemed by taxes through 1764, and in August it authorized an additional £125,000 to be redeemed by taxes through 1765.[44]

In 1762 the commissioners of the Cherokee trade received authorization to issue certificates up to £6,000 proclamation money (£4,500 sterling, or £31,500 South Carolina currency) to facilitate the trade. Although not designated as public orders, these certificates seem to have been in the same category, for they could be received in payment of all taxes and duties.[45]

Twice the province used public orders to finance construction projects. In April 1767 the scheme was used to provide £60,000 for the building of an exchange and customs house and a new watch house for Charles Town, to be redeemed within five years out of the fund from additional duties on wine, rum, and flour products.[46] Finally, in April 1770, the amount of £70,000 was issued to cover the costs of building courthouses and gaols (almost always misspelled *goals* by Carolinians) in the backcountry, as authorized by the Circuit Court Act of the previous year. This issue was to be canceled within five years by receipts from the general duty.[47]

TAX-ANTICIPATION CERTIFICATES

Another form of tender available to the province was the certificate of indebtedness issued by the public treasurer to creditors of the government when the accounts were approved and the tax bill passed. The certificate not only served to show what sum would be paid the creditor when the taxes were actually collected but also could be used by the creditor in payment of his own taxes. Although the certificate was not *legal* tender, the creditor could transfer the certificate by endorsement to another person, who would have the same privilege. Possession of the certificate would relieve the creditor of the necessity to find the same amount of money in other currency with which to pay the taxes. The certificates were supposed to be presented for payment within a few years of issue, as most of them were, but it is apparent that they were honored regardless of their age. A report on currency in 1775 listed as still in circulation certificates dated as early as 1753.[48] According to one authority, the certificates were provided "during the latter part of the colonial period," and according to another they were issued from 1750 to 1769.[49] But the practice dates from at least as early as 1736, for Gabriel Manigault, then public treasurer, was ordered by the Assembly to provide such certificates.[50]

Near the end of the colonial period, the Assembly used the tax-indebtedness certificate as an emergency device to put money into circulation. Because of the dispute over the contribution made by the Commons House to aid John Wilkes,[51] there was no agreement upon a tax bill after the one approved in August 1769. The indebtedness of the province was considerable, and there seemed little likelihood that the impasse could be broken. But in 1774 the Assembly ordered all the public accounts audited, as in previous years when tax bills had been passed, and interest-bearing certificates issued to creditors with the promise that they would be paid out of the next taxes to be collected. They were not legal tender, but they were accepted by the patriots and even by royal officials as paper money.[52] A similar issue was made in June 1775.[53]

UNOFFICIAL ISSUES AND COUNTERFEITS

In addition to the official issues, there were some unofficial issues. In 1730 a group of seventeen merchants and seven or eight planters formed a society to issue promissory notes on the principle of the land bank. Using a capital of £10,000 in bills of credit and their own credit standing, they issued £50,000 of notes, at 10 percent interest, which were accepted by the people as currency although they had no legal standing.[54] Some persons doubted the wisdom of such a private currency, and Chief Justice Benjamin Whitaker charged that the issuers had every intent to deceive or to defraud.[55]

There were some who plainly sought to defraud by defying the warning printed on many issues of colonial paper currency: "To Counterfeit is Death." There are several known spurious issues of South Carolina currency, most emanating in all likelihood from the same group of counterfeiters. The engraving and printing of colonial bills were often of such poor quality that expert counterfeiters could easily match or even surpass the efforts of the official printer. South Carolina bills were no exception. It is entirely possible that some counterfeiters were never discovered and that their creations may have entered the currency supply as perfectly acceptable items.

In June 1735 it became known that certain bills of the 1731 issue were being counterfeited, and the Assembly passed an act against counterfeiting which provided for the death penalty without benefit of clergy.[56] Commissioners were originally appointed to exchange the denominations of £15, £4, and £3, but by a later proclamation of the lieutenant governor they were to exchange the £10 denomination also.[57] One Thomas Mellichamp was sentenced to death in May 1736 for forgery and counterfeiting of £1 bills, so he does not appear to have been responsible for the other counterfeits.[58] A few years later, the Assembly considered what to do toward redeeming two types of counterfeit issues, one made illegally from the genuine plate and one made from a bogus plate. The commissioners for exchanging the currency recovered and destroyed £920 of bills made from the genuine plate and £2,147 made from the false plate.[59] It appears that the only other known counterfeiting was of the £1 bill in the issue of July 25, 1761.[60]

THE PROBLEM UNRESOLVED

South Carolina never achieved what it considered a satisfactory solution to the currency problem. Although the Commons House denied, in answer to a suggestion from England, that gold and silver could be used as the sole medium of trade in the province,[61] it toyed several times with the idea of putting the Treasury on a specie basis. In 1754 it ordered Jacob Motte to convert all his balances into foreign gold and silver coin at current values and to keep the balances in cash whenever possible.[62] On several other occasions, it authorized the public treasurer to receive any duties in foreign coins.[63]

The natural tendency, however, would have been for South Carolina to seek a solution at the other extreme, to issue paper money. The province did try on at least two occasions to make positive additions to the currency supply, only to have the statutes fail for lack of approval in England. South Carolina strongly opposed the parliamentary limitations on paper currency issues. When the Currency Act of 1751 was being considered, the Commons House carried on an extensive correspondence with the colonial agent, James Crokatt, urging him to try to get an exemption for South Carolina. Crokatt predicted rightly that the act would not include South Carolina, but he also said "that he had reason to believe no more American Acts for issuing Paper Currency . . . will ever obtain the Royal Assent. . . ."[64]

The Currency Act of 1751 restrained only the New England colonies from issuing paper money which was given legal-tender status. A new act of 1764 was applied to all the American colonies. After the passage of the Currency Act of 1764, South Carolina instructed the new colonial agent, Charles Garth, to work for its repeal, or, if it could not be repealed, for permission to make limited issues of legal-tender paper currency. But the effort met with no success. In fact, the authorities in England took steps to repeal the act which emitted £106,500 in 1769 merely to exchange the old worn bills and which did not add to the money supply at all.[65]

The currency acts, it should be noted, did not create a currency problem for South Carolina—the province had not been able to make a new legal-tender issue since 1723—but they certainly hindered attempts to provide a satisfactory currency. The province managed to struggle along with its £106,500 of paper bills, the various issues of public orders, and the tax-anticipation certificates. How precarious the system was can be gauged by the monetary crisis after 1769 when no new tax-anticipation certificates were being issued. By early 1774 the currency shortage was so severe, despite attempts to add to it by overvaluing foreign coins and by other schemes, that James Laurens reported to his brother Henry, "Mr Manigault himself complains..."[66]; and Gabriel Manigault was reputed to be one of the wealthiest men in the province.

Currency problems in themselves could hardly have precipitated the Revolution in South Carolina. But their weight was added to the burden of other grievances which the province blamed on the British government.

NOTES

[1]*Statutes*, IX, 779.
[2]Commons House Journal, October 22, 1771, XXXVIII, Part Three, 571. Even the Treasury had difficulty retaining coins, for these had completely disappeared by 1775. Provincial Congress Journal, November 18, 1775, *The State Records of South Carolina: Extracts from the Journals of the Provincial Congresses of South Carolina, 1775–1776,* ed. William E. Hemphill and Wylma Ann Wates (Columbia, 1960), 134.
[3]*Statutes*, II, 163; IX, 779; Curtis P. Nettels, *The Money Supply of the American Colonies Before 1720* (New York, 1934), 241, 248.
[4]Commons House Journal, May 9, 1752, XXVII, Part Two, 497–98.

⁵Peter Manigault to Daniel Blake, March 10, 1771, "The Letterbook of Peter Manigault, 1763–1773," ed. Maurice A. Crouse, *South Carolina Historical Magazine,* LXX (1969), 188; Commons House Journal, October 22, 1771, XXXVIII, Part Three 571.

⁶Commons House Journal, March 22, 1745/6, June 10, 1746, *The Colonial Records of South Carolina: The Journal of the Commons House of Assembly, September 10, 1745–June 17, 1746,* ed. J.H. Easterby (Columbia, 1956), 178, 212–16; R.S. Yeoman, *A Guide Book of United States Coins* (29th rev. edn.; Racine, Wisconsin, 1975), 18–21. The coins were not very popular with Americans generally. Massachusetts even printed parchment notes in denominations of 1d, 2d, and 3d to compete with Wood's money as small change. Eric P. Newman, *The Early Paper Money of America* (Racine, Wisconsin, 1967), 134.

⁷Henry Laurens to Henry Peronneau and Benjamin Dart, November 27, December 20, 1771; April 10, 1772, Letterbook, 1771–1772, 73–74, 124, 243–45, Henry Laurens Papers, South Carolina Historical Society.

⁸*Statutes,* II, 37; IX, 772–73.

⁹The paper money issues of all the colonies are described in detail, with many illustrations, in Newman, *Early Paper Money.* A good discussion of the paper money question may be found in Converse D. Clowse, *Economic Beginnings in Colonial South Carolina, 1670–1730* (Columbia, 1971), 144–55, 196–97. Richard M. Jellison, "Paper Currency in Colonial South Carolina: A Reappraisal," *South Carolina Historical Magazine,* LXII (1961), 134–47, discusses the motives behind the issues to 1731. Jellison's "Antecedents of the South Carolina Currency Acts of 1736 and 1746," *William and Mary Quarterly,* 3d series, XVI (1959), 556–67, continues the discussion to 1746.

¹⁰*Statutes,* II, 202–212; IX, 766.

¹¹*Ibid.,* II, 302–7, 320–23, 324–27, 352–54, 366; ix, 767–69.

¹²Ibid., IX, 769.

¹³Ibid., 759–65.

¹⁴Manuscript Act 354, S.C. Dept. of Archives and History (some acts were omitted deliberately, some accidentally, from Cooper and McCord's edition of the *Statutes*); *Statutes,* II, 634–41, 662–76; IX, 770–72.

¹⁵*Statutes,* IX, 772–74.

¹⁶Ibid., 775.

¹⁷Ibid., 775–76.

¹⁸See Smith, *South Carolina as a Royal Province,* 241–74, for an extended account of the struggle.

¹⁹*Statutes,* IX, 776.

²⁰Ibid., III, 305–7.

²¹Ibid., 423–30.

²²Commons House Journal, March 5, 1736/7, *JCH, 1736–1739,* 291–320.

²³*Statutes,* III, 671–78; Richard M. Jellison, "Antecedents of the South Carolina Currency Acts of 1736 and 1746," *William and Mary Quarterly,* 3d series, XVI (1959), 561–66.

²⁴*Statutes,* III 702–4; IV, 312–14.

²⁵Ibid., III, 775–76; IV, 154–55.

²⁶Ibid., III, 413.

²⁷Ibid., 334–41.

²⁸Smith, *South Carolina as a Royal Province,* 273. Smith further notes that this

issue of public orders was not fully redeemed until 1750. Alexander Parris, the Public Treasurer, did not cancel the orders as they were received by him in payment of duties.

[29]Commons House Journal, January 18, 1734-5, *JCH, 1734-1735*, 30.

[30]Commons House Journal, March 25, 1735, ibid., 128-33.

[31]Commons House Journal, April 25, 1735, ibid., 189.

[32]Commons House Journal, June 3, 1735, ibid., 224-25.

[33]Commons House Journal, January 23, March 2, 1737/8, *JCH, 1736-1739*, 404-20, 501.

[34]Council Journal, January 7, 1752, XVIII, Part Two, 533-36.

[35]*Statutes*, III, 461-64.

[36]Commons House Journal, September 18, 1738, *JCH, 1736-1739*, 585.

[37]Commons House Journal, November 25, 1742, *JCH, 1742-1744*, 59; March 9, 1754, XXIX, 194-95. Statements issued by the Commons House about the retirement of issues of public orders cannot be taken seriously in all cases. It reported in 1764 that all series of orders issued through 1760 had either been sunk already or would be sunk by the current tax act. Eleven years later there were still substantial numbers of six of those series still in circulation. Commons House Journal, August 8, 1764, XXXVI, 216-19; March 1, 1775, XXXIX, 2d pagination, 244.

[38]*Statutes*, III, 547-49.

[39]Ibid., 577-79.

[40]Ibid., 595-97.

[41]Ibid., 653-56.

[42]Manuscript Act 835.

[43]Manuscript Act 866. Newman, *Early Paper Money*, 305, gives the total as £238,300 for some unclear reason.

[44]*Statutes*, IV, 113-28, 144-48.

[45]Ibid., 168-73.

[46]Ibid., 257-61.

[47]Ibid., 323-26.

[48]Commons House Journal, March 1, 1775, XXXIX, 2d pagination, 244.

[49]Smith, *South Carolina as a Royal Province*, 278; Newman, *Early Paper Money*, 305.

[50]Commons House Journal, May 29, 1736, X, 32. Similar orders are recorded on March 5, 1736/7, March 25, 1738, *JCH, 1736-1739*, 289, 568; December 15, 1739, May 9, 1740, *JCH, 1739-1741*, 123, 340; March 6, 1741/2, *JCH, 1741-1742*, 482; May 6, 1743, *JCH, 1742-1744*, 453; May 19, 1744, *JCH, 1744-1745*, 163; June 4, 1747, *JCH, 1746-1747*, 323; and by indirection, June 28, 1748, *JCH, 1748*, 383. It is likely that the certificates were issued with every tax act after 1733.

[51]See Chapter VI, and Jack P. Greene, "Bridge to Revolution: The Wilkes Fund Controversy in South Carolina, 1769-1775," *Journal of Southern History*, XXIX (1963), 19-52.

[52]Commons House Journal, March 24, 1774, XXXIX, 2d pagination, 162-64.

[53]Commons House Journal, June 1, 1775, ibid., 287.

[54]Newman, *Early Paper Money*, 302, says the issue was never made because the capital was not paid in, but Commons House Journal, March 5, 1736/7, *JCH, 1736-1739*, 309-10, indicates that it was made. Moreover Benjamin Whitaker, *The Chief Justice's Charge to the Grand Jury for the Body of this Province* (Charles Town,

1741), 25, describes the design of the notes and says of the bankers: "From a real or imaginary Deposit of 10,000 £. in Paper Bills of Credit they acquired to themselves an annual Income of about 40 or 50 per Cent."

[55]Whitaker was engaged in political controversy when he wrote about the issue and may not be trustworthy. However, this is almost certainly the scheme which the young merchant Gabriel Manigault, soon to be public treasurer, refused on principle to join. Gabriel Manigault II to Joseph Manigault, September 13, 1808 (second letter of this date), Manigault Family Papers, South Caroliniana Library, University of South Carolina, Columbia. The younger Manigault was writing from memory and some of the details seem to be wrong.

[56]*Statutes*, III, 411–13.

[57]*South-Carolina Gazette*, June 14, July 26, 1735.

[58]Ibid., March 27, May 8, 1736. He and three other suspects had been jailed on suspicion but had escaped earlier, in September 1735. Ibid., September 27, 1735.

[59]Commons House Journal, January 27, February 3, 1737/8, March 25, 1738, *JCH, 1736–1739*, 433, 460, 563; May 9, 1740, *JCH, 1739–1741*, 339.

[60]Newman, *Early Paper Money*, 306. The known instances of counterfeiting of South Carolina's currency are therefore few. When the Assembly passed an act against counterfeiting in 1775, the act was directed against the counterfeiting of the currencies of neighboring provinces, particularly Virginia. *Statutes*, IV, 335–36.

[61]Commons House Journal, December 15, 1752, XXVIII, Part One, 141.

[62]Commons House Journal, May 10, 1754, XXIX, 382.

[63]Commons House Journal, May 9, 1752, XXVII, Part Two, 497–98; October 18, 1771, XXXVIII, Part Three, 565.

[64]Commons House Journal, December 14, 1749, XXV, Part One, 170–71; January 29, 1750/1, XXVI, Part One, 62–63.

[65]Commons House Journal, June 24, 26, 1766, XXXVII, Part One, 2d pagination, 175–76, 182; Charles Garth to Committee of Correspondence, November 24, 1770, "Garth Correspondence," ed. Theodore D. Jervey, *South Carolina Historical and Genealogical Magazine*, XXXIII (1932), 118; Joseph Albert Ernst, *Money and Politics in America, 1755–1775* (Chapel Hill, 1973), 106–14, 215–20.

[66]James Laurens to Henry Laurens, March 9, 1774, Letters of James Laurens on Domestic Subjects, 1772–1775, Henry Laurens Papers, South Carolina Historical Society, Charleston.

CHAPTER III

Import and Export Duties

SOME GOVERNMENTAL EXPENSES of the province were of a continuing or recurrent nature. There were always ministers of the Church of England to be paid, church buildings to be constructed, and fortifications to be built and kept in repair. Since the expenses were certain to occur every year and were fairly predictable as to amount, the concept of funding was applied to them. That is, the revenues derived from a continuing source such as an import duty would be designated particularly for a purpose, such as paying the clergy's salaries or sinking the various issues of public orders. The unpredictable or incidental expenses would then be paid by the levying of a general tax. This rule was by no means invariable, however. Often surpluses from the duty funds would be used to reduce the amount of the annual tax, and on occasion (as during wartime, when defense costs were especially high) the tax would be used to offset deficits in the duty funds. Transfers from one duty fund to another were common.[1]

THE NATURE OF THE PROVINCIAL DUTIES

The duties levied by South Carolina were of two basic types: those on imports and those on exports. But because of the way that the public treasurer kept the accounts after 1735, it is perhaps better to say that there were more than two types. The accounts were set up on the basis of a general duty, an additional duty (generally on rum, wines, and provisions) for the building of fortifications or public buildings, a second additional duty on rum either for defense or for church buildings, a duty on slaves, a duty on the exportation of deerskins, a duty on the exportation of tanned leather, a duty on goods imported by transients, and a duty on imported flour for the encouragement of local flour milling. The purpose for which the money was to be spent was the basis for setting up the accounts. For example, the duty on slaves was usually levied along with the general duty but was treated as a separate account because it was designated for separate purposes, such as sinking public orders or subsisting new immigrants to the province. Table 1 gives the several duty acts, their dates of effectiveness, and the general nature of the acts.

Table 1 suggests what is confirmed by a closer examination of the duty acts: the specific duties were levied on a limited number of categories of articles, chiefly alcoholic beverages, foodstuffs, wood products, animal skins, and slaves. But within those categories the duty acts typically listed many separate items by name; there were approximately eighty overall, though not all occurred in any single act. Those which were listed were taxed a definite duty regardless of their value; those which were not listed paid an *ad valorum* duty.[2]

The specified procedure differed somewhat from one duty act to another, but the basic principles for complying with the requirements remained much the same throughout. The law required that duties be paid before goods could be loaded or unloaded,[3] but this requirement was probably not enforced very strictly. Jacob Motte in 1752 listed £7,149 1s 8d due him from merchants for payment of their duties.[4] In 1767 the firm of Middleton, Liston, & Hope owed £28,000.[5] In 1773 various merchants owed £127,674 6s 11d.[6] Anyone who wished to clear port with duties goods—chiefly furs and skins—aboard had to give to the comptroller (before 1703, to the secretary of the province or to a magistrate) a list of the goods, the names of the shippers, the name of the vessel, and the name of its captain. The comptroller then made an entry in his records and gave a copy to the owner with a certification that an entry had been made. The owner took the certificate to the public receiver, paid the required duties, and received his loading permit. Before the vessel sailed, the captain had to deliver to the public receiver a list of all the cargo he was

Table 1 Import and Export Duties
Levied by the Province of South Carolina

KIND OF DUTY	ENACTED	TERMINATED	REFERENCE
Skins and furs exported	September 26, 1691	March 16, 1695/6	*Statutes*, II, 64–68
Liquor, tobacco, and provisions	Unknown	November 16, 1700?	Ibid., 96
Liquor, tobacco, and provisions	July 16, 1695	November 16, 1700	Ibid.
Skins and furs exported	March 16, 1695/6	May 6, 1703	Ibid., 110–12, 156, 162, 190
Liquor and provisions	November 16, 1700	May 6, 1703	Ibid., 162, 190
Beer and ale	March 1, 1700/1	May 6, 1703	Ibid., 177–78, 190
Drink, provisions, wood, skins, and slaves	May 6, 1703	June 30, 1716	Ibid., 200–206, 247, 308, 322, 354, 659
Liquor and other goods	November 10, 1711	June 30, 1716	Ibid., 366, 659
Negro slaves imported from Africa	December 18, 1714	June 30, 1716	Ibid., VII, 367; II, 660
Negro slaves imported from other colonies	February 18, 1714/5	June 30, 1716?	Ibid., II, 622
Drink, provisions, wood, skins, and slaves	June 30, 1716	March 20, 1718/9	Ibid., 649–61
Drink, provisions, wood, skins, slaves	December 11, 1717	March 20, 1718/9	Ibid., III, 27–30
Drink, provisions, wood, skins, and slaves	March 20, 1718/9	July 24, 1719;[a] July 28, 1721[b]	Ibid., 56–57, 68–69, 103, 122

Continued

Table 1—*Continued*

KIND OF DUTY	ENACTED	TERMINATED	REFERENCE
Rum	December 9, 1720	May 25, 1745	*Statutes*, III, 363, 653–54; Manuscript Act 630
Drink, provisions, wood, skins, and slaves	September 21, 1721	February 23, 1722/3	*Statutes*, III, 159–61
Drink, provisions, wood, skins, and slaves	February 23, 1722/3	Continued to at least 1728, probably to 1740	Ibid., 194–96, 270–71, 334–41
Wine, rum, molasses, flour, and sugar	April 9, 1734	June 14, 1751	Manuscript Act 576; *Statutes*, III, 535, 587, 646; Ledger B, 34
Goods imported by transients	December 18, 1739	Continued until Revolution	*Statutes*, III, 535; IV, 74–76; Publick's Ledger, 1771–1776, 6.
Drink, provisions, wood, skins, and slaves	April 5, 1740	June 14, 1751	*Statutes*, III, 556–68, 670

Rum	May 25, 1745	June 14, 1751	Ibid., 653–56
Drink, provisions, wood, skins, and slaves	June 14, 1751	Parts repealed April 18, 1769, August 23, 1769, April 7, 1770[c]	Ibid., 739–51; IV, 39, 264–65, 322, 332
Wine, rum, biscuit, and flour	July 6, 1757	June 2, 1761?	Ibid., IV, 150
Wine, rum, biscuit, and flour	June 2, 1761	April 18, 1767?	Ibid., 150–51
Slaves	August 25, 1764	December 31, 1768	Ibid., 187–88
Wine, rum, biscuit, and flour	April 18, 1767	Continued until Revolution	Ibid., 257–61; Publick's Ledger, 1771–1776, 10
Flour	March 20, 1771	Continued until Revolution	*Statutes*, IV, 329; Publick's Ledger, 1771–1776, 5

[a]Declared invalid by Proprietors.
[b]Re-enacted and extended to date given.
[c]Remainder continued to at least 1772; extended to 1776.

transporting so that it could be ascertained that the duties had actually been paid on all dutied goods. If everything were in order, the public receiver would then grant permission to sail.[7] A very similar procedure, except for sailing clearance, was required before dutied goods could be imported and unloaded.[8]

To ensure compliance with the duty laws, the public receiver and other officials were authorized to receive information on oath and to search vessels if they suspected false information (giving false information or interfering with a search subjected the violator to a fine of £100). Armed with a warrant from a justice of the peace (perhaps an early-day "writ of assistance"?) the officials could search houses and other buildings for smuggled goods, which could be confiscated if found within three months of the time the duties were supposed to have been paid.[9]

The duty laws were, of course, not always complied with. A bit of cheating is suggested by the title of an act of December 18, 1713: "An Act to prevent wines the growth of the Western Islands to be imported into this Province as wines of the growth of Madeira. . . ." Since Madeira was duties at a much lower rate than the other wines, there was an obvious incentive for cheating by mislabeling. To prevent it, the act required a certificate of origin on all wines which entered as Madeira.[10]

Goods imported into South Carolina were taxed if they were on the duty list regardless of the importer's intent to re-export them, though the duty laws specified that under certain conditions all or a part of the duties could be refunded. Such a refund was called a drawback, and the Treasury issued a certificate of credit called a debenture instead of making a cash payment (the debenture could be used in payment of the next duties which were incurred by the holder). If a vessel put into harbor in distress because of weather conditions or damage to the vessel, the whole amount of the duty could be remitted. If a perishable cargo spoiled, the owner could ask for a total remission of duties, and up to 10 percent could be allowed routinely for leakage of liquid cargo. If duties goods were re-exported, usually within a time limit of six months, from one-half to three-fourths of the duty would be refunded.[11] Re-exporting was fairly common. For example, for the period ending December 31, 1768, when the collections amounted to £16,778 os 10d, debentures were issued to the amount of £1,819 2s 1d.[12]

Preferential rates were often given under the duty acts to encourage the development of local shipping. The most favorable treatment was extended by the act of 1717 which admitted goods without payment of any duties at all if they were carried in vessels which had been built in South Carolina and were wholly owned by residents. If the vessels were built in the province but owned by nonresidents, the goods were taxed one-half the stated duties. And if the vessels had been built elsewhere but were owned by residents of South Carolina, the goods were taxed three-fourths the stated duties. The act had such repercussions in England that the proprietors invalidated it early in 1719.[13] Later acts were less favorable but still gave some preference to local citizens.

The British authorities did not like another feature of the early acts which subjected British goods to the duties. In 1718 the proprietors ordered the repeal of one of the acts on the grounds that the Crown had objected to such taxation. Later acts either specifically stated that British goods were exempted, as in 1721 when only the additional duty on rum (for building St. Philip's church) was levied on them, or noted that the duties applied only to produce of America or "the plantations."[14]

THE GENERAL DUTY

First in the broadness of its application but not necessarily in the revenues derived therefrom was the general duty act.[15] The number of duty acts and the number of articles contained in each prevent an easy explanation of the historical development of the duties. Table 2 uses the act of June 14, 1751, as a standard by which to compare an early act (May 6, 1703) and an intermediate act (February 23, 1722/3).

It must be remembered that the duties were stated in current money. In 1703 the South Carolina currency was fairly close to being at par with sterling. By 1721 it took £4 currency to equal £1

Table 2 Comparison of the Duty Acts
of 1703, 1723, and 1751

ITEM	UNIT	DUTY PER UNIT		
		1703	1723	1751
Madeira wine	Pipe	£3	£6	£8
Canary, Fiall, or Vidonia ("Western Islands") wine	Pipe	£5	£10	£10
Rum	Gallon	3d	4d	1s 3d
Northern beer	Barrel			10s
Northern cider	Barrel		10s	5s
Molasses	Gallon	1d	3d	5d
Brandy or spirits (except rum)	Gallon	1s 3d	2s	2s
Brown or Muscovado sugar	Hundredweight	1s per hundredweight	2s 6d	5s
Clayed sugar	Hundredweight	on all sugar	5s	7s 6d
Refined sugar	(Varies)		3d per pound	4d per pound
Cocoa	Hundredweight	2s 6d	1s 3d	£2
Chocolate, made-up	Pound		1s	1s
Tobacco	(Varies)		1s 3d per hundredweight	3d per pound

Item	Unit			
Butter	Hundredweight		10s	£1
Tallow	Hundredweight		7s 6d	£1
Pork	Barrel		£1 10s	£2
Beef	Barrel		10s	10s
Brown or ship biscuit	Hundredweight	1s 3d	1s 3d	2s 6d
Midling biscuit	Hundredweight		3s 9d	3s 9d
White biscuit	Hundredweight	2s 6d	2s 6d	5s
Flour	(Varies)	2s 6d per hundredweight	2s 6d per half barrel	3s 9d per hundredweight
Bacon	Hundredweight		£1	£1 10s
Soap	Hundredweight		£1	£1
Timber, planks, boards, staves, shingles, and lumber	£100 prime cost		£20	£20
Indian slave	Each		£50	£50
Deerskin	Each	3d	6d	6d
Tar, pitch, and turpentine	Barrel		£1	£1
Peas and Indian corn	Bushel		1s	1s
Indigo	Pound		1s	1s
Whalebone	Pound		1s	1s 6d

References: *Statutes*, II, 200–1; III, 194–95, 744. Only the dutied items listed in the act of 1751 are included here.

sterling, and by 1751 it took £7 currency. Allowing for depreciation, the duties of 1751 were usually lower than those levied at the beginning of the century.

The general duty fund was used primarily to pay the salaries of the clergy, church clerks, and sextons, and masters of the Free School. Because salaries were increased several times and many new parishes were created, those expenses increased rather greatly over the years, from £8,607 17s ¾d in 1735 to £18,752 9s 8d in 1773.[16] The duty act of 1751 made several allotments from the fund because it was producing much more than needed for the above purposes, and the money could better be used elsewhere. Each year the fortifications fund received £5,000; £1,500 went to build a new church (St. Michael's parish had recently been created by dividing St. Philip's parish); £200 was to be used for building a parsonage house in St. Michael's; and £2,500 went toward building a new state house.[17] Beginning in June 1761, presumably because that part of the act of June 1751 had expired, St. Michael's received no more of the allotment.[18] In 1770 the act which authorized the building of jails and courthouses specified that the £70,000 issue of public orders would be retired from the general duty fund at the rate of £14,000 a year.[19]

For accounting purposes the duties on exported deerskins and on exported tanned leather were combined with the general duty. In theory, the export duties were supposed to pay the salaries of the clergy, but if there was not sufficient income from them (and after a time they did not come even close to providing the required revenue), the general duties would be used as a supplement.[20] Animal skins and hides were the very first articles to be dutied. The duty act of 1691 taxed the export of deerskins and of exotic skins that were later of no commercial importance: beaver, otter, fox or "Catt," boar, and raccoon. Deerskins were the only items that were taxed continuously. One by one the exotic skins began dropping out of the duty lists, their places taken by new listings. The items of continuing importance were only five in number. Deerskins were taxed at rates varying between 1d and 3d between 1691 and 1723. The duty act of February 23, 1722/3, established a rate that remained in effect throughout the remainder of the colonial period. Skins weighing under a pound were taxed at 3d, those over a pound, 6d. Tanned leather was taxed at 1d per pound until 1723, 2d per pound thereafter. Tanned calfskins or tanned deerskins were always taxed at 1s each, rawhides ranged between 5s and £1 each, and neat leather ranged between 6d and 3s per side.[21]

The income from the general duty could well be regarded as an index of commercial activity. In the early years the general duty produced relatively little, perhaps £8,000 in a good year.[22] By the early 1750s the income had grown to £12,000 per year. A plateau was reached in the 1760s, when the income generally ran about £30,000 per year, with occasional spurts as high as £40,000. During the 1770s the income began dropping off, and in 1775 the fund produced only £22,312 1s 6d.

At first the export duties contributed substantially to the general duty fund. For example, when the fund received about £8,000 some £2,900 came from the export duties. But the deerskin duties, which ran about £3,800 in the 1740s, declined rather steadily after 1750, reaching a level of about £1,700 per year in the 1770s; and the tanned leather duty was never an important money-maker—it generally produced between £300 and £800 per year throughout its existence.

THE ADDITIONAL DUTY

Military emergencies would create the need for more revenue than could be supplied from the general duty or from immediate taxation. One of the customary responses to this crisis—issuing of paper money was another—was the levying of an additional duty, that is, one payable over and above the already existing duties. The first occasion seems to have been in 1711 to finance an expedition against the Tuscarora Indians.[23] In 1717 another additional duty was needed to finance an expedition to fight against the Yamassee Indians. The additional duties were levied on roughly the same group of articles as those already covered by the general duty act of 1716 and amounted to a doubling (or in the case of a few articles, more than a doubling) of the existing rates for the duration of the act.[24]

Much the same situation prevailed in the 1730s when feelings ran high between the English and the Spaniards over the founding of Georgia in disputed territory. Knowing that the defense of Georgia was necessary to the defense of South Carolina, the Assembly allotted £8,000 from its additional duty on rum for the support of the new colony. Rum was already taxed at 4d a gallon by the general duty act of 1719[25] when an additional duty act, beginning in 1720, levied 3d a gallon more for the building of a "brick church" (St. Philip's) in Charles Town.[26] In 1733 the bulk of the fund was made payable to the benefit of Georgia until such time as the sum of £8,000 should be reached.[27] Knowing that the defense of Georgia could not be relied upon as South Carolina's sole defense, the Assembly planned fortifications to ward off any possible attack by the Spaniards. For this purpose, a new additional duty was called for in 1734. This was more selective than the act of 1717, being levied only on Madeira wine, rum, molasses, flour, and sugar. On these few articles, the effective rate paid by importers was approximately doubled.[28]

This additional duty was extended by later acts until 1751 because of the continuing hostilities with Spain during the War of Jenkins' Ear and King George's War. Its termination did not mean the end of revenues devoted to fortifications. Thereafter, until the end of the colonial period, there was an account for fortifications provided either by a new additional duty or by the diversion of funds from other accounts.[29] The goal of £8,000 for Georgia from the rum duty had been reached in 1737, and thereafter, with a small amount set aside for St. Philip's church, most of the rum duty also was added to the fortifications fund. The 3d act expired in 1745; a new act doubled the rate to 6d a gallon and devoted the income entirely to fortifications. This duty also was maintained until 1751.[30]

During the years that they were posted to separate accounts (1735–45), the duty on rum produced between £1,700 and £3,000 per year, and the duty on wine, rum, molasses, flour, and sugar produced between £3,800 and £7,700.[31] The merged duties after 1745 produced £10,000 or more in a typical year.[32]

The expiration of the additional duties came at an inopportune time, when the coming of the French and Indian War caused defense costs to soar once more. Although much of the additional expense for fortifications was borne by the annual tax (the taxes for 1754 and 1755 contributed £20,000 each) or by public orders (£62,300 in 1758), once more there were additional duties levied on wine, rum, biscuit, and flour, in 1757 and again in 1761. Compared with earlier rates, these were fairly moderate. For example, a pipe of wine, depending on its variety, paid either £8 or £10 in regular duty; the additional duty was £4 10s.[33] But with the growing commerce of the province, even moderate duties were good money-makers. The new additional duties produced at least £10,000 almost every year (the prominent exception was 1766, when the effect of nonimportation was felt), and after 1768 the revenue was generally between £14,000 and £19,000.[34]

It should be noted that the fortifications fund provided only for fortifications. It did not cover other defenses such as the raising and supplying of troops, the costs of which were borne by the annual tax. (In reality, such current expenses were usually paid for by the issuing of public orders, which were then redeemed out of later taxes.)

The additional duty was not always used for defense purposes. After 1767 the proceeds went to build an exchange and customs house and a new watch house in Charles Town.[35]

THE NEGRO DUTY

The first "Negro Duty," or duty on imported black slaves, was levied by the act of May 6, 1703, which taxed any slave over eight years of age. Those coming from Africa were subject to a duty of 10s each, while those coming from other places, such as the West Indies or other continental colonies, were taxed double that amount.[36] An act of 1714 levied £2 additional duty on each slave imported from Africa,[37] and an act of 1715, no longer extant, probably made a similar or higher levy on slaves imported from other colonies.[38] The higher duties imposed on slaves from places other than Africa were made even more stringent by the acts of 1716, 1719, 1721, and 1723. In 1716 the rates were £3 for African imports and £30 for those from other places, in 1719 and 1721 they were £10 and £30, and in 1723 they were £10 and £50.[39] The justification for the higher rates on slaves from the American colonies was that "they were either transported thence by the Courts of justice, or sent off by private persons for their ill behaviour or misdemeanours,"[40] and therefore made undesirable slaves.

The act of April 5, 1740, sought to limit importation of slaves by levying a prohibitively high duty. Possibly because the earlier acts which had levied varying duties according to age (the rates previously given were for adults) had been difficult to administer (in case of dispute about age, a justice of the peace made a ruling), this act based the duties on height, a determination certainly easier to make. For fifteen months after the passage of the act, the duty levied on slaves under 3 feet, 2 inches was £2 10s; for those 3 feet, 2 inches to 4 feet, 2 inches it was £5; and on taller slaves it was £10. But for three years thereafter, the rates on each category were multiplied by a factor of ten, so that adult slaves could be subject to a duty of £100. After three years the duties returned to the previous levels. Two-thirds of the revenues were to go toward subsidizing the immigration of poor Protestants to South Carolina's backcountry.[41]

The new duty act of June 14, 1751, did not change the duties levied, but it did change the purpose for which the revenues were spent. Four-fifths of the revenue would be used to encourage the settlement of poor Protestants, and one-fifth was to go for bounties to shipwrights and caulkers to encourage the building of ships within the province.[42] In 1754 a portion was directed toward building a pesthouse (for quaranting incoming passengers who were ill) and erecting a beacon in Charles Town harbor.[43]

The duty on slaves was usually a large, although erratic, source of revenue.[44] The years 1735–40 were years of fairly heavy importation. The income averaged about £14,000, and the year 1736 alone produced £33,104 13s 7d. The importation was so heavy that an official report blamed it for many of the financial difficulties of the province.[45] And the Stono Rebellion of 1739 aroused fears of creating potentially dangerous hordes of slaves, who were judged to be of "a barbarous and savage disposition."[46]

The virtually prohibitive duties levied by the act of 1740 were very effective in reducing importation. For the years 1741–48 there was a total income of £9,569 9s 9d (£6,831 13s 3d of which was in 1744 alone), and several accounting periods saw no income at all. Even so, the fund was so large that in 1742 the public treasurer was directed to put out £7,000 at interest annually.[47] The lack of income was eventually felt, however. The fund was so low by early 1750 that the Commons House proposed that the public treasurer be allowed to issue up to £4,000 in notes similar to tax-anticipation certificates, which would be payable out of future receipts from the Negro duty and which would themselves be accepted in payment of the Negro duty. The Council rejected the idea, noting the bad impression that such a procedure would create in England and suggesting that other funds in the Treasury might be "borrowed" for the time being.[48]

Beginning in 1749 and lasting through 1758 there was a return to a level of importation only slightly below that of the 1730s. For the next three years, 1758–60, there was a remarkable rise in income from the duty, averaging about £27,000 per year. Income in the period 1761–63 was about £10,000 per year. Then followed two more years of high income: £28,993 5s in 1764 and £60,441 16s 3d in 1765. For the following three years there was practically a cessation of importation of slaves because of the levying of an additional duty of £100 per slave during that period.[49] There was another year of exceptional income in 1769 (£44,071 15s), followed by a year of practically no importation because of the South Carolina nonimportation agreements of June 28 and July 22, 1769, which barred the importation of slaves after January 1, 1770. The agreement was revoked December 13, 1770,[50] and the year 1771 began another extended period of frantic importation, reaching a peak in 1773 with an income of £77,314 15s. One observer attributed the activity in the slave market to the desire of a great number of recently arrived settlers in the backcountry to hold slaves. He wrote, "It is to these people we owe the Extravagant Price of Negroes. The great Planters have bought few Negroes within these two Years. Upwards of two thirds that have been imported have gone backwards. These people some of them come

at the Distance of 300 Miles from Chs Town, & will not go back
without Negroes, let the Price be what it will."[51]

THE MINOR DUTIES

One minor duty fund was begun in 1739 when a tax was placed
on goods brought into the harbor and sold by persons who were
not residents of the province. The duty was designed to discour-
age the practice of ship captains and other transients using
Charles Town as a market without contributing to its financial
support. The rates were established at 1 percent of the prime cost
of all articles which were not subject to any duty by the laws of
South Carolina, and ½ percent of the prime cost of all articles on
which regular duties were paid.[52] The revenue was not considerable, seldom being above £500 per year.[53] The fund was used to
help pay for the town watch, which annually required far more
money than that provided by the duty on transients and fees from
tavern licenses, the deficit being offset from the annual tax.[54]

Beginning in 1771 the province collected an additional duty of
5s per hundred pounds on imported flour, the proceeds of which
were used to pay a bounty of 10s per hundred pounds to local
producers of flour.[55] Somewhat less than £3,000 a year was
realized from this duty during its short history.[56]

TRANSFER OF FUNDS

Sirmans says that income from import and export duties was
"permanently earmarked" for specific purposes,[57] implying that it
could not be spent otherwise. This statement is quite incorrect.
Although most of the funded accounts were spent for their stated
purposes, frequently the money was used elsewhere, but always
with the Assembly's direction and approval.

After about 1740 one of the most frequent uses of duty funds
was to reduce the amount of the annual tax. The first such incidents were scattered—1721, 1733, 1738—but the province soon
came to enjoy the relief from taxation which the surpluses pro-

vided.[58] After 1742 there were only three tax acts, and after 1754 there was not a single one, which did not appropriate surplus funds from the duty accounts.

The "Fund appropriated for Building a Pest House and erecting a Beacon &ca." disbursed relatively little money for its stated purposes. Only £18,483 17s 2d was thus paid out, but £40,867 14s 8d went for other purposes, chiefly for building St. Michael's steeple and for easing taxation.[59] The account for a "Bounty for Building Ships in this Province" apparently never paid a penny in bounties. The only disbursements were to the commissary-general, to the account for the pesthouse and beacon, and in ease of taxation.[60] The title of a duty account was certainly no positive indication that the money would be spent for that purpose.

A YEAR WITH THE DUTY FUNDS

It would be useful to examine what activity might occur during a typical year with the duty funds. Since Chapter IV on taxes will use the year 1764 for illustration, the closest approximation to it that can be deduced from the duty accounts, the year beginning March 25, 1764, and ending March 25, 1765, will be used as an example.

At the beginning of the accounting period, the public treasurer showed a cash balance of £95,181 13s 11d. During the next six months, he received £40,357 4s from various sources: £15,145 11s 10d from the general duty; £6,904 8s from the additional duty; £388 18s 4d from the duty on tanned leather; £1,819 9s 6d from the duty on deerskins; £130 11s 4d from the duty on imports by transients; and £15,968 5s from the duty on Negro slaves. He made disbursements of £26,154 7s 10d, which left him a cash balance of £109,384 9s 1d.

The duties on tanned leather and deerskins were, as usual, transferred to the general duty account. That account made disbursements for two varieties of expenses. Debentures returned £1,794 15s 3d to merchants who re-exported goods on which they had earlier paid duties. The payment of salaries to the ministers of the Church of England and the staff of the Free School amounted to £6,895. There were several transfers of funds which could not be regarded as direct expenses of the general duty account. Following the duty act of 1751, the public treasurer shifted £2,500 to the fortifications fund and £1,250 to the fund for building a state house.

Direct payments from the additional duty account were all for debentures, amounting to £432 13s 1d. In addition, after the account was officially closed out, an allotment from it was made to reduce the burden of the tax act of 1765. In earlier years the duty on goods imported by transients would have been directed toward paying for the town watch, but the tax act of 1765 dipped into the balance available from the fund to reduce taxation.

The only direct charge to the Negro duty fund was a few debentures for slaves re-exported from the province, which came to £176 5s. This, however, does not reveal the full activity of the account. In accordance with the duty act of 1751, as amended in 1754, the public treasurer, after deducting a commission for handling the receipts, transferred four-fifths of the balance (£12,310 14s 3d) to the fund for new settlers and one-fifth (£3,077 13s 6d) to the fund for the pesthouse and beacon, thereby completely closing out the account.

The fund for building a parsonage house in St. Michael's parish had long since collected the £2,000 which had been appropriated to it, and £1,500 had been paid in 1757. Now the commissioners issued an order and the Treasury paid out the remaining £500.

The fortifications fund paid, upon its commissioners' orders, £1,156 10s 1d to various persons. Similarly, the public treasurer paid £1,032 16s 10d out of a fund appropriated for repairing Fort Johnson. As a matter of fact, however, that fund had not had any money in it since 1757 (the tax act of 1765 eventually provided £3,500)—another example of *pro forma* bookkeeping.

The account for new settlers was the most active account during the period. The public treasurer recorded dozens of bounties to individual settlers (mostly in amounts of £21 and £35) which totaled £6,440. The fund also paid the firm of Torrans, Gregg, & Poaug £496 2s 1d for supplies and paid £3,699 19s 4d toward the support of French Protestants who had recently arrived from

England to settle in South Carolina. The commissary-general received £1,500 for various services.

Commissions were charged to the individual funds at a rate of 2½ percent for receipts and for disbursements. In the cash account they were summarized as a total of £1701 10s.

In the next six-month period, which ended March 25, 1765, the public treasurer received £37,306 7s 1d and disbursed £24,860 9s 4d, which left a cash balance of £121,830 7s 10d. The income accounts followed very closely the pattern of the previous period. The general duty collected £14,808 7s 2d, the additional duty of £7,284 2s 6d, the duty on tanned leather £226 11s 6d, the duty on deerskins £1,554 5s 6d, the duty on imports by transients £408 0s 5d, and the duty on Negro slaves £13,025.

Nor were the disbursements radically different from the earlier period. The general duty fund paid £1,409 18s 3d in debentures. The other payments were somewhat higher than in the previous period, because they included not only the usual salaries for the clergy and the Free School (£7,405), but also parochial charges for all the parishes (£715), repairs to St. Philip's Church (£200), and back salaries to two clergymen (£405). There were the customary transfers to the fortifications and the state house accounts.

Once more the Negro duty fund's only direct expense was the payment of £52 10s in debentures, and there were the usual transfers to the accounts for new settlers and the pesthouse and beacon to close it out. The fortifications account paid £413 10s upon the commissioners' orders.

The new settlers account recorded far fewer bounties paid directly to individual settlers—only £784—but there were two payments to William Wooddrop and Andrew Cathcart, who had brought over 338 persons and who collected £10,260 3s 6d for their efforts. The commissary-general received £1,000. The other accounts were inactive. Commissions for the accounting period were stated as £1,607 14s 6d.[61]

The various duty accounts disbursed for governmental expenses during the period March 25, 1764–March 25, 1765, totaled £51,004 17s 2d. The tax act of April 6, 1765, called for the sum of £133,198 1s to be raised from taxes or the application of surplus duty funds to pay other expenses for the year 1764.[62] The two fiscal periods are not identical, but it is apparent that the total expenses of government for 1764 were approximately £184,000.

Even if the two fiscal periods had been identical, it would still be difficult to say exactly what the expenses of government were for any given period because of the haphazard way in which Jacob Motte kept his records. The balances, collections, and expenditures are those given by Motte in his books. Actually, as Motte eventually found out, the cash balances were greatly in error. The first indication that he had begun to doubt his own records came when he realized that he had not recorded his commissions on several transfers from the duty funds to the general tax as far back as 1754, and subsequently he made corrections in the general duty, additional duty, transient duty, and pesthouse and beacon accounts. (The corrections were made following the accounts for the period ending September 29, 1764, but the entries must have been made much later, for they reflect transfers which were made by the tax act of April 6, 1765—such transfers are an indication of Motte's laxness.)[63] It apparently did not occur to him at the time to make corrections in his cash account, however. Sometime after September 29, 1765, he finally realized that the cash account was in serious error. Possibly after making a careful search to ascertain the cause, he discovered fourteen different items which had to be adjusted, reducing the cash balance in his ledger by £74,082 8s 10d.[64]

THE VALUE OF THE DUTY FUNDS

The first duty act was passed to create a "publick treasure" because the lack of it had frequently caused delays in preparing forces for the defense of the province against foreign attack.[65] With the issuing of its first bills of credit in 1703, the province found a new purpose for the duty funds, that of helping to secure the bills.[66] After giving up real hope that the bills of credit could ever be redeemed, the Assembly in 1716 found a third use for the duty funds. They could be used for "paying debts due by the publick, and all other contingent charges of the government, as shall be ordered and directed by an order or ordinance of the General Assembly."[67] Eventually the Assembly saw fit to designate certain duties for continuing purposes, as in 1722 when it set aside the duty on skins and furs (and part of the general duty, if need be) for paying the salaries of the clergy.[68] Special designation soon became the rule, but the Assembly always reserved the right to remove money from the duty funds and spend it for any other purpose.

The existence of the duty funds benefited the province in two ways. First, they provided a source of income other than direct taxes, thereby reducing the taxes by perhaps one-fourth. (The duties were real taxes, but they were "hidden," as are many modern taxes, by passing them along to the consumer in the form of higher prices. Even then, higher prices probably seemed more tolerable than higher taxes.) Second, in years when taxes were for some reason not collected, as after 1769 when the Assembly could not agree on a tax bill, the duties provided enough continuing revenues to keep the Public Treasury from falling into utter bankruptcy. They were a useful cushion against the shock of fiscal disasters.

NOTES

[1]The warning given by Newton Jones in his pamphlet accompanying the microfilm version of the records of the public treasurers is well founded. One cannot assume that moneys paid out of a particular fund were applied toward the usual purposes of that fund; it is necessary to examine the accounts in some detail to see for what purposes the funds were actually disbursed.

[2]Items on which duties were imposed at some time during the colonial period included rum, Madeira wine, Vidonia wine, Fiall or Canary wine, brandy and other spirits, mumm, stout, ale, cider, ordinary wine, beer, northern cider, northern beer, peas, Indian corn, myrtle wax, beeswax, spermacetti, spermacetti oil, preserves or sweetmeats, cotton, aloes, whalebone, apples, pears, onions, indigo, soap, blubber, train oil, tallow, candles, vinegar, pimiento, pickled salmon, mackeral and herring, salt fish, flour, brown or ship biscuit, midling biscuit, white biscuit, brown or Muscovado sugar, clayed sugar, refined loaf sugar, cranberries, beef, pork, bacon, cheese, butter, cocoa, cocoa nuts, made-up chocolate, lime juice, tobacco, molasses, scraped ginger, scalded ginger, timber products, woodenware, pitch, tar, turpentine, bricks, logwood, Braziletta wood, other dyewoods, horses, Negro slaves, Indian slaves, deer skins, Indian-dressed deerskins, tanned deerskins, tanned calfskins, raw hides, beaver skins, fox or cat skins, boar skins, raccoon skins, tanned leather, and neat leather.

³*Statutes*, II, 64, 202–3, 653.

⁴Commons House Journal, December 7, 1752, XXVIII, Part One, 96.

⁵Henry Laurens to William Reeve, October 2, 1767, "Correspondence of Henry Laurens," ed. Joseph W. Barnwell, *South Carolina Historical and Genealogical Magazine*, XXVIII (1927), 213.

⁶Upper House Journal, August 11, 1773, C.O. 5/478, 6.

⁷*Statutes*, II, 64–65, 177.

⁸Ibid., 201.

⁹Ibid., 65, 203.

¹⁰Ibid., VI, 613–15. The act explains that wines from the Azores had been taxed heavily because they were thought to be harmful to health.

¹¹Ibid., II, 126, 202–3, 305.

¹²Ledger B, 79.

¹³*Statutes*, III, 32–33.

¹⁴Ibid., 30, 160–61, 744.

¹⁵South Carolina was one of three colonies (along with New York and Massachusetts) which regularly levied duties on imports. Emory Johnson, et al, *History of Domestic and Foreign Commerce of the United States* (2 vols.; Washington, 1915), I, 57.

¹⁶Journal A, 14, 34; Journal C, 739.

¹⁷*Statutes*, III, 749–50.

¹⁸Ledger B, 66.

¹⁹*Statutes*, IV, 324.

²⁰See, for example, the act of June 23, 1722, which granted £150 proclamation money to the rector of St. Philip's and £100 proclamation money to country rectors. Ibid., III, 174–76.

²¹Ibid., II, 64, 100, 201, 650; III, 160, 195, 562, 744–45.

²²All remarks about income and expenditure from the general duty fund are based on Ledger B, 3, 12, 14, 18, 29, 33, 40, 47, 50, 55, 60, 66, 71, 74, 79; Publick's Ledger, 1771–1776, 1, 15.

²³The act is not extant, but the title is given in *Statutes*, II, 366.

²⁴Ibid., III, 23–30.

²⁵Ibid., 56.

²⁶The act is not extant, but the title is given in ibid., 111.

²⁷Ibid., 363.

²⁸Manuscript Act 576.

²⁹*Statutes*, III, 587, 646.

³⁰Manuscript Act 630; *Statutes*, III, 587, 653–56.

³¹Ledger B, 5, 9, 22; 4, 17, 20–21, 27.

³²Ibid., 27, 34.

³³*Statutes*, IV, 150–51. The act of 1757 is not printed, but the 1761 act indicates that the former is probably a re-enactment of the earlier law.

³⁴Ledger B, 59, 69, 77; Publick's Ledger, 1771–1776, 4.

³⁵*Statutes*, IV, 259.

³⁶Ibid., II, 201. A supplementary act of 1706 makes it clear that slaves already belonging to a resident, but who were being employed elsewhere, could be brought into South Carolina without the payment of any duty, unless they were resold within a year. The importer had to post bond that the slaves would not be sold within that period. Ibid., 280. For an extended treatment of the Negro duty, see W. Robert Higgins, "A Study of the South Carolina Negro Duty Law, 1703–1775" (master's thesis, University of South Carolina, 1964). In addition to the tax on black

slaves, the province levied a tax of £5 on Indian slaves in an act of 1719. The chief tax on Indian slaves was on those exported: 20s in 1716, £20 in 1721, £50 in 1723 and all later acts. *Statutes,* II, 650; III, 57, 160, 194, 562, 744.

[37]*Statutes,* VII, 367.

[38]Ibid., II, 622.

[39]Ibid., 651; III, 56–57, 160–61, 194–95.

[40]Ibid., III, 195.

[41]Ibid., 557.

[42]Ibid., 739–42. Three-fifths would be used to pay bounties directly to the settlers on a graduated basis, the later arrivals to receive correspondingly smaller bounties. One-fifth would be used for making surveys and grants of land to the settlers. There is no record that any of the remaining portion actually went toward bounties to shipbuilders; it appears that all of it was eventually used for poor Protestants, too.

[43]Ibid., IV, 10–11. From 1757 through 1759, the pesthouse and beacon account was designated to assist in the building of St. Michael's Church, the parsonage, and a state house. Ibid., 38–41. Although it is not immediately obvious, it was funds derived from the Negro duty that were being used for those purposes.

[44]All remarks about receipts and disbursements are based on Ledger B, 6, 11, 21, 24, 30, 39, 56, 70; Publick's Ledger, 1771–1776, 7.

[45]Commons House Journal, March 5, 1736/7, *JCH, 1736–1739,* 312.

[46]*Statutes,* III, 556.

[47]Council Journal, May 22, 1742, VIII, 48.

[48]Commons House Journal, January 31, February 7, 1749/50, *The Colonial Records of South Carolina; The Journal of the Commons House of Assembly, March 28, 1749–March 19, 1750,* ed. J.H. Easterby and Ruth S. Green (Columbia, 1962), 371, 394.

[49]*Statutes,* IV, 187–88.

[50]*South-Carolina Gazette,* July 6, 27, 1769; December 13, 1770.

[51]Peter Manigault to William Blake, undated but *circa* December 17–24, 1772, "Letterbook of Peter Manigault, 1763–1773," ed. Maurice A. Crouse, *South Carolina Historical Magazine,* LXX (1969), 191.

[52]*Statutes,* III, 535–36.

[53] Ledger B, 15, 35, 65, 82; Publick's Ledger, 1771–1776, 6.

[54]*Statutes,* III, 536.

[55]Ibid., IV, 329.

[56]Publick's Ledger, 1771–1776, 5.

[57]*Colonial South Carolina,* 242–43.

[58]*Statutes,* III, 149, 352, 510.

[59]Ledger B, 53; Publick's Ledger, 1771–1776, 12.

[60]Ledger B, 44.

[61]Ibid., 42–43, 52–54, 68–73; Journal B, 401, 404–5, 407–8, 423, 425–27.

[62]*Statutes,* IV, 214.

[63]Ledger B, 53, 65, 69, 74.

[64]Ibid., 75.

[65]*Statutes,* II, 64.

[66]Ibid., 211.

[67]Ibid., 658–59.

[68]Ibid., III, 174.

CHAPTER IV

Taxes

THE EXPENSES OF GOVERNMENT which were not funded by the import and export duties were paid by the levying of a tax. Some of the early statutes are not extant, but it appears that until about 1715 taxes were levied at irregular intervals as the need for funds arose. There is no record of any taxation at all between 1704 and 1713. If the province hoped that the issues of bills of credit backed by import and export duties which began in 1703 would eliminate the need for taxes, that hope was visionary. The need to redeem new bills from tax funds, coupled with the need to raise money to prosecute the Yamassee War, caused taxation rates to rise remarkably in 1715. Thereafter, there were usually annual taxes except in politically chaotic years such as 1728–30 and 1770–76, when the Assembly either did not meet or refused to approve a tax law.[1]

A YEAR WITH THE TAX ACCOUNTS

Using the tax act of April 6, 1765, as a basis for discussion, it is possible to follow a typical year's taxation. The process started long before the passage of the act. As early as October 1764 the newspaper began carrying the advertisement by the clerk of the Commons House that in accordance with a resolution of July 20, 1764, no accounts for indebtedness would be considered unless received within twelve months of the date of the service performed. Two weeks later Jacob Motte, as public treasurer, placed an advertisement requesting that all public creditors bring in their accounts, attested by oath, before January 1, 1765. As the deadline for submission of the accounts approached, both advertisements appeared again.[2]

Early in January, Lieutenant Governor William Bull remarked in his address to the opening session of the Assembly: "The Public Treasurer is ordered to lay before you the accounts of Debts for Various Public Services for the last year, that you may make Provision for the discharging of them." The remark was routine, as was the Commons House's reply: "The Public accounts for the Various services of the last year, your Hono'r may depend shall meet with all the Consideration and Dispatch, That His Majesty's Honor and our Duty to our constituants require."[3]

Motte presented the Commons House with 144 numbered accounts and petitions for payments of debts incurred through the end of 1764. Rawlins Lowndes, the speaker, apppointed a committee of nine members to audit them and bring in an estimate of the charges for which the government would be responsible. He also appointed a committee of six members to audit the accounts of the public treasurer to ascertain what balances might be in the various accounts that could be applied toward reducing the amount of the tax.[4]

The committee on public accounts deliberated for seven weeks before making its recommendations on the first group of accounts and a week longer before reporting on the remainder. The committee had gone over the accounts with great care, for it saw reason to raise objections to thirty-five of them, recommending that some be paid only in part and that others not be allowed at all. Several of the accounts were for expenses not authorized by the Assembly; some were for expenses that had already been paid, or should be paid from other funds; and others were deemed to range from "vagen and uncertain" and "unus'al & improper" through "very Extravigant" to "very exorbitant, & . . . unsupported, by any proof." Christopher Howe was, in effect, accused of writing out receipts to himself to prove the province's indebtedness to him for an expedition to Long Canes.

Another militia account was rejected with the notation, "The com'ee know no right, that the Militia have to charge, their Tavern Bills to the Public." The committee found it impossible to decide on the legitimacy of several accounts and appealed to the judgment of the full House. One concerned John Hume's account for cleaning the ordnance of the province:

> The Com'ee observe that this is the first charge against the Public for cleaning Cartouch boxes, and submit it to the House, whither Mr. Miller who is a Gunsmith by Trade and as always Served the Public faithfully, ought not to have the preference, in cleaning the arms, and whither the Salary voted by this House to the Ordinance Store Keeper, was not intended in full for his Services, without any allowance to him for an overseer.[5]

The full House accepted nearly all the recommendations of the committee, rejecting only three.

At the morning session of March 15, 1765, Lowndes appointed a committee of three members to draft a tax bill. The committee on accounts was instructed at the same time to report a schedule of charges which would be appended to the bill. This meant nothing more than categorizing the usual expenses of government and inserting the special accounts, which had just been audited, in their proper places. To speed up the legislative process, the first committee reported back at the afternoon session with the skeleton of a tax bill (with blanks in the places calling for tax rates), which received the first of three required readings. The second committee presented for a first reading on March 26 its schedule of charges, which was annexed to the tax bill.[6] By March 29 the tax bill was nearing definitive form. On its second reading, it called for the raising of £102,927 12s 3d by taxation and the applying of £30,270 8s 9d from various funds in the Treasury.[7] The bill then went to the Council, which reported that it had read the bill two times and was returning it to the Commons House. After a few minor changes, the bill was read the third time and sent to the Council. On April 6 the Council reported that it had approved the bill on its third reading. The bill was then engrossed, taken to the Council for examination, and the Great Seal attached to it. Later in the day the speaker notified the Commons House that the lieutenant governor had given his assent, and the bill became law.[8]

The £133,198 1s appropriated by the tax act covered a wide variety of expenses. First in the schedule came the salaries of public officers: the lieutenant governor, clerk of the Council, master in chancery, messenger to the Council, doorkeeper to the Council, clerk of the Assembly, messengers of the Assembly, commissary-general, clerk of the board of church commissioners, public treasurer (this was for miscellaneous commissions; he received most commissions from the duty funds), colonial agent in Great Britain, clerk of the committee of correspondence, and ordnance storekeeper, for a total of £7,874 7s 10½d. House rent for the governor, the lieutenant governor, and the Free School came to £950. Writing and printing for the public amounted to £5,207 13s 2½d. Payments made in accordance with various directives of law, mostly the sinking of the two issues of public orders of 1760, totaled £75,048 12s 6d. There were several categories relating to defense costs; forts and garrisons, £7,507 16s 6d; public arms and ordnance stores, £883 19s 1d;[9] private frontier forts, £334 19s 10d; rangers £4,124 9s 5d; supplies for the forces, £2,275 7s 6½d; supplies for scouts from the militia, £110 11s; and supplies for scout boats, £55 6s 3d. Parochial charges for St. Paul, St. Helena, St. Stephen, and St. Mark parishes totaled £5,500 (those were special charges; each parish usually got about £40 annually from the general duty fund for routine charges). Coroners' inquests required £185 15s.[10] Indian expenses, chiefly entertainment of visiting Indians, were £510 17s 2d. Three categories concerned expenses for criminals: fees, subsistence, and conveyance costs were £4,209 10s 7½d; compensation for criminal slaves executed, £1,130; and constables' fees on trials of slaves, £224 12s 6d. Caretakers' salaries and maintenance costs for public buildings required £3,481 14s 9d. Charles Town proper was expected to raise £1,914 15s in a special tax to cover costs of fire engines, fire buckets, and expenses of the commissioners of roads and commissioners of streets. Finally, extraordinary expenses, such as running a boundary line between North and South Carolina and making bounty payments on hemp, required £11,668 2s 9d.

Over the years the lawmakers had learned to judge fairly well how to produce the desired revenues by the application of certain rates to the taxable items. The act of 1765 provided that Negro and other slaves would be taxed at 17s 6d each; land, except for town lots, 17s 6d per hundred acres; town lots, wharves, buildings, and other town lands, 8s 9d per £100 value; bonds and other evidences of money let at interest, 8s 9d per £100 (in a rather modern way, the act allowed this tax to be offset by the amount of interest paid by the same person); annuities, £1 15s per £100; free Negroes, mulattoes, and mestizoes aged 10 to 60, not otherwise taxed, 17s 6d each; stock-in-trade (wares, merchandise, book debts of traders and storekeepers), 8s 9d per £100; profits from faculties (physicians were commonly called "the faculty" in the eighteenth century), professions (except the clergy), factorage, and handicraft—a kind of income tax—8s 9d per £100. Exempted from any taxes were the lands of new settlers who had been in the province less than ten years, and all property devoted to pious or charitable uses.

Although the total tax was no longer prorated between Charles Town and the country according to a formula, there was still a very real distinction in the way the taxation process proceeded in the two areas. Outside the city parishes of St. Philip and St. Michael, all persons subject to the tax were required to deliver a sworn or affirmed statement in writing to the inquirers and collectors before January 1, 1766, setting forth a list of taxable property. Taxes were then to be paid by the first Tuesday in April, and the collectors would transmit the taxes to the public treasurer before the first Tuesday in May, after deducting a commission of £2 for every £100 collected. Within the city the inquirers would visit every house, after giving a three-week notice of their intentions in the *South-Carolina Gazette,* to compile a list of all taxable property, carefully identifying that which was outside the town limits and subject to the country tax. The inquirers would turn over their lists to the assessors before the first Tuesday in February. The assessors in turn would post a notice at the guardhouse, giving persons a chance to examine the listings and raise objections if they thought they were being overrated. By a sworn statement a person could have his rating reduced by the assessors. The assessors would then begin the task of calculating the taxes which were payable by each person, a process which was to be finished by the last Tuesday in April. After giving two notices in the *Gazette,* the assessors were to post a copy of their calculations at the guardhouse for inspection. The assessors would then assume their role as collectors and collect the tax by the last Tuesday in May, take their commission of £1 per £100 collected, and transmit the proceeds to the public treasurer. Collectors reported their own property and paid their taxes directly to the public treasurer.

The act contained elaborate provisions to ensure that the tax was actually paid by all those who were subject to it. Anyone who failed to deliver his property statement on time could be subjected to twice the stated rates.[11] If a person in the country attempted to conceal any of his property, he could be penalized by a fine five times as great as the tax on the property. Absentee owners of country property were required to have trustees or attorneys pay their taxes or be subjected to several possible penalties. After giving proper notice in the *Gazette* the collectors could lease the lands or sell the timber to recover the taxes, or the lands could be declared forfeited after two years of nonpayment of taxes. Town dwellers who failed to comply with the tax requirements could be subjected to double rates, seizure and sale of their goods, or imprisonment until such time as the tax should be paid. If the giver of a mortgage did not pay his taxes, the mortgagee was liable for them. If a person died before paying the assessed taxes, none of his estate could be disposed of until the taxes were collected. A person who left the province after the assessment of taxes had either to pay the taxes before his departure or find someone to guarantee that the taxes would be paid at the scheduled time. All officials involved in the tax process, including the law officers who might have to make arrests for noncompliance, were subject to a fine of £50 proclamation money if they did not perform their duties; assessors and collectors, the most important officials, were subject to a fine of £300 proclamation money.[12]

Because editor Peter Timothy would not use the stamps required by the Stamp Act, the *South-Carolina Gazette* suspended publication at the end of October 1765, making it impossible for the required notices to be placed in it at the proper times. But Charles Crouch had begun a new newspaper with the notation "NO STAMPED PAPER to be had," and the tax officials placed their notices in it. In late December, Caleb Lloyd, William Fair, and Joshua Lockwood, the inquirers for the parishes of St. Philip and St. Michael, gave notice of their intention to begin visiting houses on the first Tuesday in January 1766 to receive returns of taxable effects.[13]

In April, John Lloyd, William Savage, John Snelling, George Bedon, and Benjamin Baker advertised that as assessors and collectors they would post the required calculations at the guard-house on Tuesday, May 6, and for ten days thereafter. Then they would sit at Elisha Poinsett's house from ten to twelve and from three to five o'clock daily to receive complaints from those persons who thought themselves overrated.[14]

Shortly afterward, the newspaper carried the notice that the time for paying taxes had been extended.[15] The Assembly had passed an act on March 15, 1766, granting an extension for country taxpapers to the first Tuesday in December 1766 and those within Charles Town to the last Tuesday in January 1767. The reason given for the extension was that "many causes have lately concurred to make it extremely inconvenient and difficult to his Majesty's faithful subjects of this Province, to pay the taxes imposed on them by the tax Act...."[16] Doubtless the disturbances over the Stamp Act had something to do with the extension.

Although the Assembly could, and rather often did, extend the deadlines for filing returns or paying taxes, it frowned upon any extension granted by anyone else. Jacob Motte was once reprimanded with the reminder that the tax act gave him no discretion to give indulgence to any of the collectors, and for several years in a row the Commons House indirectly censured Motte by noting that it could not balance the tax accounts because several parishes and districts were late in reporting—it was the public treasurer's duty to issue warrants against anyone who delayed.[17]

When the returns of the tax act of April 6, 1765, covering the expenses of 1764, were audited on July 22, 1769,[18] they revealed that £113,114 17s 3d had been collected through the regular collectors; £30,270 8s 9d had been taken, in accordance with the tax act, from various duty funds; Elisha Poinsett had collected the stipulated £1,914 15s from Charles Town in a special tax; and there were six small payments of taxes directly from individuals, most for arrears of taxes. The total available was £145,339 9s 9d.

The greater part of the tax record consisted of an accounting for the tax certificates that had been issued. The record was practically identical with the schedule of charges contained in the tax act,[19] but for unstated reasons a few of the certificates had not been issued, so that instead of the £133,198 1s authorized in the act, only £132,866 10s 10d had been issued. The proceeds from the taxation were further reduced by the commissions given to the collectors. The country collectors, who were entitled to 2 percent of their collections, received £1,287 4s 2d; the town collectors, who were entitled to only 1 percent, got £487 10s 10d; and Poinsett also got 1 percent, or £19 2s 11d, for his efforts. Still there was a surplus of £10,679 1s, which was to be applied against the tax for charges of the year 1768.[20]

Table 3, derived from the tax record, gives the taxable property and the amount of taxes raised from each district.[21] By far the larger part of the revenues came from the tax on slaves.[22] Out of the total of £113,114 17s 3d raised by the tax, the tax on slaves accounted for about £63,500. The next most productive source of revenue was the tax on country lands, amounting to about £24,300. Then in order of their importance came the taxes on money at interest, £11,800; lots in towns, £10,635; faculties, professions, and stock in trade, £4,800; value of country stores, £410; and free Negroes, £103 5s. The residents of Charles Town paid £48,754 8s 5d, or about 43 percent of the total tax when their holdings in the country were added to those in town. On town holdings alone, residents paid slightly more than 25 percent of the total tax.[23]

THE PROCESS OF TAXATION

The process of taxation used in the 1760s was a far cry from the methods which had first been used in the colony. The earliest extant tax act, passed in 1686 before there was a Public Treasury as such, depicts a system so rudimentary that the two receivers of the tax were expected to give personal notice to each taxpayer of the amount he was expected to pay.[24] There were minor changes with each tax act, but until 1716 the procedure was roughly as

Table 3   Tax Returns
under the Act of April 6, 1765

PARISH OR DISTRICT	NEGROES (NUMBER)	FREE NEGROES (NUMBER)	VALUE OF LOTS (£)	LANDS (ACRES)
Christ Church	1,661			44,093
St. James, Goose Creek	2,200	1		79,103
Upper part of Goose Creek	128			9,732
St. John, Berkley	2,700	8		115,290
St. George, Dorchester	2,954	6	7,410	69,326
St. Thomas and St. Dennis	2,147		260	68,107
St. Andrew	1,977		2,450	67,774
James Island	976			15,545
John's Island	1,545			33,402
Wadmelaw Island	495	4	200	9,370
Edisto Island	939			18,602
St. Paul, say Stono	3,797			102,474
Beach Hill	957			22,923
St. Bartholomew	3,168		9,150	69,562
Upper district of St. Bartholomew	82	14	100	3,795
Combahee & Cheehaw	1,580		1,020	34,615
St. James, Santee	1,762		190	55,927
St. Stephen	1,889			62,334
Prince George	4,404	9	45,926	179,452
Welch Tract	1,016	4		68,192
Prince Frederick	3,318	5	1,500	134,192
St. Mark	1,650			121,041
St. Helena	4,162		18,750	149,195
St. Peter	756	4	2,220	44,932
Prince William	2,292	12	1,320	63,066
New Windsor Township	325	3		21,789
Amelia Township	220			9,795
Orangeburgh Township	512		50	39,206
Saxe Gotha Township	730	5		73,605
Broad River	89	2		15,550
Forks of Broad and Saludy	249			47,484
Charles Town	6,078	41	2,328,450	
Charles Town, in the country	15,811		11,850	699,158
Totals	72,569	118	2,430,846	2,548,631

Reference: General Tax, Receipts and Payments, 1761–1769 (1771), 90.

Table 3—*Continued*

MONIES AT INTEREST (£)	VALUE OF STORES (£)	PROFITS FROM FACULTIES, PROFESSIONS STOCK IN TRADE (£)	AMOUNT OF TAXATION £	s	d
24,157			1,944	17	6
24,027		5,737	2,755	9	10
		170	197	17	11
38,341	9,500	4,921	3,609	2	5
61,150	6,300	11,990	3,577	5	1
44,319		7,001	2,700	4	5
23,993	2,000	3,790	2,463	19	4
17,907		1,624	1,082	9	3
61,397		1,400	1,919	4	3
7,500		900	556	4	10
27,181	100	1,143	1,108	19	6
23,804		1,580	4,330	14	5
8,074		1,550	1,081	2	5
16,296	10,300	10,600	3,585	3	4
110		1,450	124	9	4
449	6,500	2,880	1,793	12	1
21,751		5,823	2,152	11	5
55,316		3,087	2,453	16	2
17,042	21,100	25,380	5,910	8	4
947	5,500	150	1,519	8	7
37,615	500	6,655	4,286	2	11
1,415	200	1,850	2,528	17	10
17,922	22,500	1,300	5,212	13	2
475	500	1,310	1,079	9	4
2,999	6,000	2,600	2,625	12	1
	1,000		488	19	10
			278	4	1
2,895	1,900	350	846	14	10
4,313		400	1,314	8	2
			197	7	6
			634	18	8
2,099,977		989,700	28,565	2	3
56,274			20,189	6	2
2,697,646	93,900	1,095,341	£113,114	17	3

follows: After the passage of a law authorizing taxation of the "estates, stocks and abilities" of the province's inhabitants, inquirers would prepare lists of taxable property—usually neat cattle, horses, sheep, swine, white servants, slaves, lands, and buildings—which would be turned over to the assessors. The assessors would determine the amount of tax each person would have to pay, based on his taxable property, to produce the expected revenue. The public receiver would then, either personally or through deputies such as the militia captains, inform each person of his tax. (Beginning in 1715, the tax lists would be posted on the parish church door or in some other public place for inspection.) If anyone thought that he had been overrated, he could appeal to the commissioners of appeal, who had authority to make adjustments as they saw fit. On a given day the taxes were supposed to be paid in Charles Town to the public receiver.[25]

The act of June 30, 1716, made several important additions in the interest of better collection of taxes, without changing the basic procedure. Because of the Yamassee War, the province had found it impossible to collect some £60,000 which had been levied the year before, and funds were badly needed. This seems to have been the first time that taxpayers were required to give a sworn statement of their property. The act was intended to draw the bulk of funds from taxing land and slaves, and if some provision had not been made to prevent it, Charles Town would have escaped much of the taxation. To make sure that Charles Town paid its fair share, it was assigned the definite quota of one-fifth of the total tax, which was to be assessed on the customary "estates, real and personal, stocks and abilities."[26] The quota system remained in effect until 1758.

Essentially a new system of taxation came into being with the act of February 15, 1723/4, although there had been some foreshadowings of the changes in the acts of previous years. The fundamental difference was that instead of relying on the cumbersome technique of assessment to raise the country tax, definite rates of taxation were applied: 5s per hundred acres of land and 15s per slave.[27] Almost as important was the stipulation that instead of being visited by an inquirer, each country taxpayer would have to deliver a written, sworn statement of his property to a new official called the collector or receiver and pay the amount of tax for which his property made him liable. A trip to Charles Town by the taxpayer was no longer necessary. In one trip, the collector would take all the funds which he had collected within his district and make his settlement with the public treasurer. The process was much shorter and simpler than before. It required fewer officials and less time to collect a given tax. However, the Assembly did not feel capable of devising a definite schedule of taxation for town property, and within Charles Town the old system of using inquirers, assessors, and collectors to collect the town's quota was retained.[28] Charles Town's density of population made the procedure easier to follow there than in the country areas.

In 1731 the Assembly tinkered, with unfortunate results, with the system which it had created in 1724. For its first taxation measure since 1727 the Assembly returned partially to the assessment system for the country tax, levying 20s on each slave and then assessing land for the remainder. First, the date for collecting had to be extended because of a failure to communicate the act's provisions to the populace. Then, some districts still did not report, and the inquirers in others thwarted the purpose of the assessment by reporting all lands at identical values.[29] In the next tax act, that of June 3, 1733, there was a definite return to specific rates of taxation.[30]

An important innovation came in 1733. In previous acts, the Assembly had attempted to anticipate many expenses and to levy taxes in advance of them. No tax laws had been passed between 1727 and 1731, however, and although the tax law of 1731 anticipated expenses, a separate law authorized the issuing of public orders to pay off the backlog of debts.[31] The technique of paying off past debts rather than trying to anticipate future liabilities must have been an attractive one, for it was adopted in 1733 (ratified on June 7, 1733, the law covered debts for the period March 25, 1732–March 25, 1733) and used constantly thereafter.[32] The government no longer made immediate payment of debts but required that creditors submit accounts which would be paid out of the next tax. Because taxation was for expenses already incurred, the tax act could call for a very precise amount of money to be raised.

Along with the tax act, the Assembly usually directed the public treasurer to issue certificates to the creditors, indicating the amount of the province's indebtedness and promising payment out of the taxes to be raised under the act.[33] (The public orders of 1731 were analogous, but they promised payment from a duty fund instead of from taxes.) The issuing of the tax certificates formalized a practice which had been hotly disputed at the beginning of the century. In 1703 the Commons House learned that several persons had refused to pay their taxes, claiming that the province owed them more than the amount of their tax. The Commons House did not at the time approve of a "Discount," or the offsetting of taxes by a credit for sums due a person from the province.[34] Governor Nathaniel Johnson was critical of that position, and the Commons House finally agreed to allow the offsetting.[35] The tax certificates were a complete "Discount" in a sense—with each year's law enough tax certificates would be generated to pay off every farthing of the tax. In effect, goods and services were offset by taxes, or vice versa. In receiving the tax certificates, the public treasurer was not really receiving money. On the other hand, when the certificates were returned in payment of taxes, he did not have to pay out any money; he was merely accepting the return of a statement of the province's liability and canceling it. (All this presumes, of course, that taxation actually brought in at least as much as the expenses of the government.) It is probable that few government creditors held on to their certificates long enough to pay them into the Treasury for taxes owed under the act which issued them. It was usually a year, and sometimes longer, from the time that the tax act was passed until the taxes were collected. In the meantime the holder of the certificate probably would have used it to pay his previous year's taxes or have transferred it to someone else in payment of a private debt. The original recipient need not be the person who finally presented it for redemption, and the certificate could circulate for a while before being redeemed. The system of tax certificates was one which obviated the need for much other currency, and indeed the certificates served very usefully as a real addition to the currency supply of the province.

Between 1733 and 1758 the changes in the tax laws were

numerous, but they can be summed up under a few headings. First, the division of taxes between Charles Town and the rest of the province was modified. In 1741 the town's share was reduced from one-sixth to one-tenth because of the disastrous fire of 1740.[36] The Assembly concluded the next year that Charles Town's proper share thereafter should be one-fifth of the total tax,[37] and so it remained as long as the quota system was issued. Second, the Assembly exempted certain kinds of property from taxes. Beginning in 1735, new settlers in the province did not have to pay taxes on their land for the first ten years.[38] After 1739 the lands and slaves owned by the churches and the free schools did not bear taxation.[39] However, the Assembly was always in search of new sources of revenues and created many new categories of taxable items.

The last major change in taxation procedures came in 1758 when the Assembly abandoned the quota system and devised a definite schedule of taxation even for town property, making the task of the town assessor very simple and allowing his office to become essentially that of collector, with which it was indeed merged.[40] The procedure had by this time become that which was described in detail at the beginning of this chapter.

THE SEARCH FOR SOURCES OF REVENUE

The early tax acts usually called for assessment of the "estates, stocks and abilities" or "the estates, goods and merchandize, stocks and abilities, also of money by them, or in money lying at interest, in any person's hand."[41] It seems unclear exactly what was understood by "abilities," but it is apparent that the stress of early taxation was upon the two items which were first singled out for specific rates of taxation: land and slaves. Not only were they the first to bear specific rates, but they also furnished the bulk of the revenue throughout the colonial period. Earlier taxation generally relied more heavily on revenues from slave owners, but after 1744 the rate was always the same on a hundred acres of land as on a single slave.[42] The rate of taxation varied, of course, with the amount of money to be raised. Land was usually taxed between 5s and £1 per hundred acres and owners between 10s and £1 for each slave. In war years the rates were much higher. In 1760 the rates rose to £1 15s on each item, and in 1761 they stood at £2 10s, the highest rates ever charged.[43]

Country storekeepers early attracted the attention of the Assembly. By 1719 the law provided that they should pay the same rates as storekeepers in Charles Town, but their payments would count toward the country quota. Beginning in 1734, the country storekeepers were taxed by a definite rate.[44] The tax began at a level of £2 for every £100 of stock and cash. It rose to £3 in 1740 and fell sharply thereafter, never being more than 11s 3d per £100 through 1757. After that date, country storekeepers and Charles Town storekeepers were taxed identically. Taxation rates were already rising in 1757 because of the war, and storekeepers had to pay up to £1 5s per £100 before the rates fell back to normal at the war's end.

Money at interest was probably always considered as a taxable item, but it was singled out for a specific rate in the country tax only in 1740.[45] Over the years when it was listed as a taxable item (through 1758), the rate ranged from 5s to 11s 3d per £100. The province began listing bonds, specialties, and notes as taxable items in 1745 [46] with rates the same as those on money at interest, so it does not appear that there was any distinction among these items for taxation purposes. Under the newer classification, money on loan was taxed at the same rate as stock in trade, profits from trades and professions, and town property, all of which reached the high level of £1 5s per £100 in 1761, but were much lower in peacetime. Annuities were related to money at interest but were taxed much more heavily. They were first taxed specifically in 1752 at £1 10s per £100[47] and remained at that level while money at interest was taxed only 5s per £100. The wartime level was £5 per £100.

It is possible that income from employment was comprehended under "abilities" and so taxed from the very beginning. The very earliest acts definitely taxed the income of public officials,[48] and for a brief period in the 1740s the officials were taxed at a specific rate, 3 percent or slightly higher.[49] Profits from the trades, factorage, faculties (physicians), and professions (except the clergy) were mentioned in a description of the assessment for Charles Town in 1753[50] and continued thereafter, being taxed at a specific rate after 1758. If this was not the same as the modern payroll or income tax, it was very similar in concept. Although those who paid it probably thought the tax was exorbitant, it was scarcely higher than 1 percent even in wartime and was generally much less than that.

The earliest taxes may have come rather close to being poll or head taxes, but the poll tax proper was never widely used. The province attempted such a tax on white males, at the rate of £1 or less, during the years 1734–37, but it was never used again. It was probably a very unpopular tax. Beginning in 1756, however, a head tax was levied on free Negroes who paid no other tax. The rate was always identical with that levied on slave ownership, but because of the few persons involved, it produced negligible revenue.

In its search for revenue, the Assembly levied one very odd tax in 1757 and 1758: a rate on "black cattle, [that is to say] upon all calves, exceeding thirty in number, raised, marked, branded or sold by any person in one year."[51] Whether this was thought of primarily as a taxation measure or as a regulation of the cattle industry is unclear. It does not seem to have been used again.

Just as South Carolina anticipated the income tax, it also used something similar to the surtax. This tax was not calculated as an additional percentage of an existing tax, but the effect was about the same because it was levied on the same property. In 1717, during the Indian wars, the Assembly called for £17,000 over and above the £30,000 already levied for collection in March 1717/8, and £5,000 over in March 1718/9. In 1755, another war year, the Assembly levied additional taxes on a schedule that added one-eighth to the already existing rates.[52]

As could be expected, the amount raised by taxation tended to rise over the years. The early taxes were for exceedingly small sums, usually £450 or £500 sterling. By the 1720s the acts usually sought to raise between £20,000 and £30,000 currency. In 1750 the amount went over £60,000 for the first time; in 1757 it exceeded £100,000, followed in 1758 by more than £166,000. The all-time high was reached in 1761 with a tax of £284,757 17s 4¾d.

After that, the level fell off sharply and the last tax act, passed in
1769, was for only £70,326 7s 2d. (As indicated in Chapter III,
many governmental expenses were paid from the duty funds; the
total annual budget was much larger than would appear from
taxation alone.)

Collections did not always meet expectations. During the
Yamassee War, for example, it was impossible to collect two taxes
of £30,000 each, and the province was forced in 1716 to levy
£95,000, to be collected in three annual installments, to make up
for losses and to pay current expenses.[53] For the period for which
there is detailed information (1761–69), it appears that the legislators had learned to gauge fairly accurately how much money
could be raised by any given rate of taxation. Table 4 gives the
relationship between expected and actual collections.[54] The Assembly overestimated its income about as often as it underesti-
mated it, but for the period as a whole the tax produced slightly
more revenue than anticipated.

THE BURDEN OF TAXATION

Lord North, speaking of all the American colonies in 1775, said
that the average Englishman paid 25s in taxes annually, but the
average American paid only 6d—a ratio of fifty-to-one.[55] There is
ample testimony from contemporaries that the rate of taxation in
South Carolina was fairly low in peacetime,[56] but the rates were
certainly higher than 6d per person. The relatively great wealth
of South Carolinians[57] caused their taxes to be higher than those
of many other colonists; at the same time, it made payment easier.

Just how heavily did the burden of taxation fall upon South
Carolinians? The taxes varied so much from time to time that a
meaningful average is difficult to ascertain. Speaking generally, it
appears that taxation became easier to bear with each passing
decade, and by the 1760s it was no special burden to the average
South Carolinian. The taxes raised during the Yamassee War of
the mid-1710s was especially onerous when considered on a per
capita basis. The act of 1716 taxed some five or six thousand white
persons for £35,000 in a single year and followed that sum by

Table 4 Expected versus Actual
Tax Collections, 1761–69

YEAR LEVIED	EXPECTED			ACTUAL			SURPLUS OR (DEFICIT)		
1761	£284,757	17s	4¾d	£263,844	8s	11d	(£20,913	8s	5¾d)
1762	£162,120	11s	3½d	£161,550	3s	9d	(£570	7s	6½d)
1763	[No tax act was passed in 1763; the act of 1764 was for the expenses of two years.]								
1764	£220,307	7s	3d	£246,396	17s	1d	£26,089	9s	10d
1765	£102,927	12s	3d	£115,029	12s	3d	£12,102	0s	0d
1766	£35,529	17s	1d	£50,842	10s	0d	£15,312	12s	11d
1767	£85,950	2s	5d	£105,443	3s	2d	£19,493	0s	9d
1768	£105,773	9s	6d	£100,890	0s	5d	(£4,883	9s	1d)
1769	£70,326	7s	2d	£64,833	6s	7d	(£5,493	0s	7d)

References: *Statutes*, IV, 189–206, 214–28, 238–54, 268–83; Manuscript Acts 909, 925, 979, 990; General Tax, Receipts and Payments, 1761–1769 (1771), 39, 54, 77, 90, 107, 126, 145, 164–65.

taxes of £30,000 for each of the two following years.[58] Per capita levies of £5 and £7 (£2½ to £3½ sterling) must have seemed intolerable to a society which was still in its early stages of economic development. The distress is indicated by provisions made in several tax laws that taxes could be paid in rice or even in barrels if money were lacking.[59] But those were unusually difficult times.

In 1742 the Assembly made a determination of the province's wealth, so definite correlations may be made between wealth and taxes for that period. Working with the figures given by Eugene Sirmans, one concludes that the per capita wealth at the time was about £100 sterling.[60] The tax covering the expenses of government for 1742 levied approximately 7s sterling per capita.[61] If it can be assumed that earnings were about 6 percent of the total wealth, then the rate of taxation in 1742 was almost exactly the 5 percent of income which Governor Glen gave as his high estimate.[62]

The burden quite naturally became heavier during the French and Indian War. The highest tax ever levied, £284,757 17s 4¾d in 1761 to pay expenses for 1760, resulted in per capita taxation of £7 15s, or slightly more than £1 sterling.[63] But the end of the war brought lower rates. The last tax, levied in 1769, if distributed equally among the white population would have come to only £1 9s, or 4s 2d sterling.[64]

South Carolina, then, was not the taxpayer's paradise that Lord North imagined. Still, it seems certain that relative to the ability to bear taxation South Carolinians were usually lightly taxed. It was not local taxation nor even taxation by Parliament that stirred rebellion within the province; it was rather the struggle for control of the levying and appropriation of the taxes.

NOTES

[1]Whitney, *Government of the Colony of South Carolina*, 97, and Lawrence H. Gipson, *The Coming of the Revolution* (New York, 1954), 149–50, both give the impression that South Carolina often did not pass tax laws because the money was not needed. In *The British Empire Before the American Revolution*, vol. XI: *The Triumphant Empire: The Rumbling of the Coming Storm, 1766–1770* (New York, 1965), 541–79, Gipson presents a more accurate account of the political controversies that caused tax bills to fail of passage, although the money was desperately needed.

[2]*South-Carolina Gazette,* October 1, 15, December 10, 1764.

[3]Commons House Journal, January 8, 11, 1765, *Journal of the Commons House of Assembly of South Carolina, January 8, 1765–August 9, 1765,* ed. A.S. Salley (Columbia, 1949), 6, 10.

[4]Commons House Journal, January 15, 1765, ibid., 12–20.

[5]Commons House Journal, March 5, 13, 1765, ibid., 50–60, 75–79. Hume was paid for cleaning the arms, but not for cleaning the cartouche boxes or hiring an overseer. Commons House Journal, March 13, 1765, ibid., 81.

[6]Commons House Journal, March 15, 26, 1765, ibid., 90, 92, 103.

[7]Commons House Journal, March 29, 1765, ibid., 112. The committee had obviously coordinated its work with the committee on the public treasurer's accounts, which reported shortly that £30,270 8s 9d was available for application. Commons House Journal, April 2, 1765, ibid., 121–24.

[8]Commons House Journal, April 1, 3–4, 6, 1765, ibid., 119, 129–34.

[9]General Tax, Receipts and Payments, 1761–1769 (1771), 82; *Statutes,* IV, 225, added incorrectly or miscopied the figure as £883 9s 1d.

[10]General Tax, Receipts and Payments, 1761–1769 (1771), 84; Statutes, IV, 226, again added incorrectly or miscopied the figure as £185. But Commons House Journal, following entry of August 9, 1765, *JCH, 1765,* 172, gives the figure as £185 5s.

[11]See General Tax, Receipts and Payments, 1761–1769 (1771), 109–12, for such a fine.

[12]*Statutes,* IV, 214–28.

[13]*South-Carolina Gazetteer; and Country Journal,* December 24, 1765. By the time the second and third notices appeared on December 31, 1765, and January 7, 1766, Crouch had changed the name of his newspaper slightly, to *South-Carolina Gazette; and Country Journal.*

[14]Ibid., April 8, 15, 22, 1766.

[15]Ibid., May 20, 27, 1766.

[16]*Statutes,* IV, 234–36.

[17]Commons House Journal, June 5, 1747, *JCH, 1746–1747,* 333; January 23, 1747/8, *JCH, 1748,* 19; April 28, 1750, xxv, Part Two, 523; March 13, 1750/1, xxvI, Part One, 229; April 17, 1752, xxvII, Part One, 316.

[18]The audits of the tax records were performed very irregularly. Apparently taxes for the years 1759, 1760, 1761, 1762, and 1763 were all audited at the same time. Although undated, the same statement in the same handwriting appears on all of them, and the balances of all were applied toward easing the tax for 1767, so they were probably audited sometime in 1768. Records for 1764 and 1765 were audited July 22, 1760; for 1766, on February 28, 1770; for 1767 and 1768, on August 16 and 17, 1773. General Tax, Receipts and Payments, 1761–1769 (1771), 39, 54, 77, 90, 107, 126, 145, 164.

[19]This particular account has no check marks, but accounts for other years indicate that the public treasurer literally checked off the certificates as he issued them.

[20]General Tax, Receipts and Payments, 1761–1769 (1771), 89–90.

[21]I have tried, without success, to find a consistent pattern to the order in which the taxation districts were listed. In a rough way, the districts were listed by county, and by backcountry areas, but there were enough discrepancies to make one wonder if there really was a systematic order of listing.

[22]Because the totals are not given in the accounts, they must be calculated. I

have checked and rechecked my calculations, but they simply will not add up to the exact total given in the account. (There is no column for annuities; perhaps that explains the difference.) Therefore I am giving approximate values for the sums produced by taxation. They are close enough to the actual yields for any practical purposes.

[23]No firmly based deductions may be made about the relative wealth of the districts because the table does not indicate where residents of Charles Town held their country property. It is apparent that the taxes paid by the parishes which neighbored Charles Town would have been greatly magnified if they had included the taxes paid by town residents who owned property in them.

[24]*Statutes*, II, 16.

[25]Ibid., 182–85, 206–12, 627–33.

[26]Ibid., 662–76.

[27]The acts from 1716 onward had generally placed a definite rate on land, with the remainder of the tax to be raised by assessment of the value of slaves. The act of 1720 had definite rates on both, but the act of 1721 went back to the earlier system. Ibid., 671; III, 37, 40, 112, 149.

[28]Ibid., III, 206–14.

[29]Ibid., 308, 318, 320.

[30]Ibid., 353.

[31]Ibid., 334–41.

[32]Ibid., 359, 362.

[33]Commons House Journal, May 29, 1736, x, 32. The certificates were probably issued every year after 1733, but I have not found any documentation for years prior to 1736.

[34]Commons House Journal, January 20, 1702/3, *JCH, 1703*, 15.

[35]Commons House Journal, March 7, 1705/6, April 1, 1706, *JCH, 1706*, 10, 46.

[36]Manuscript Act 689.

[37]Commons House Journal, March 3, 1741/2, *JCH, 1741–1742*, 458–60.

[38]C.O. 5/414, 14.

[39]*Statutes*, III, 528.

[40]Ibid., IV, 53–73.

[41]Ibid., II, 16, 628.

[42]Where specific references are not given for observations made in this section, it will be understood that I have derived the information from a tabulation of all the tax acts which I have located, the sources for which are *Statutes*, II, v, 15–18, 23–25, 36–37, 62, 77, 182–85, 189, 206–12, 229–32, 259, 618, 627–33, 662–76; III, 34–38, 39–41, 69–84, 112–15, 149–57, 206–14, 238–45, 257–65, 308–17, 352–62, 383–93, 438–48, 472–84, 502–13, 527–41; IV, 53–73, 128–43, 189–206, 214–28, 238–54, 268–83; Manuscript Acts 673, 688, 689, 696, 712, 724, 739, 755, 767, 770, 780, 792, 818, 829, 835, 856, 865, 888, 909, 925, 979, 990; C.O. 5/412, no. 80; C.O. 5/414, 14–21; *Acts Passed by the General Assembly of South-Carolina, . . . [from] the Fourteenth Day of November, . . . 1751 . . . to the 16th Day of May, 1752* (Charles-Town, 1753), 35–36.

[43]*Statutes*, IV, 129; Manuscript Act 909.

[44]*Statutes*, III, 386.

[45]Manuscript Act 673.

[46]Manuscript Act 724.

[47]*Acts Passed by the General Assembly of South-Carolina, . . . [from] the Fourteenth Day of November, . . . 1751 . . . to the 16th Day of May, 1752* (Charles-Town, 1753), 35.

[48]*Statutes,* II, 16, 183.

[49]Manuscript Acts 724, 739, 755.

[50]Manuscript Act 818.

[51]*Statutes,* IV, 54; Manuscript Act 865.

[52]*Statutes,* III, 36–37; Manuscript Act 835.

[53]*Statutes,* II, 663–64.

[54]The figures are for taxation only; they do not reflect any funds made available by transfer from the duty funds. They include the special levies on Charles Town for town expenses, but not late collections of taxes.

[55]John C. Miller, *Origins of the American Revolution* (Boston, 1943), 89.

[56]See, for example, "John Tobler's Description of South Carolina (1753)," ed. Walter L. Robbins, *South Carolina Historical Magazine,* LXXI (1970), 161, and David Ramsay, *The History of South Carolina, From its First Settlement in 1670, to the Year 1808* (2 vols.; Charleston, 1809), I, 114.

[57]Carl Bridenbaugh, *Myths & Realities: Societies of the Colonial South* (New York, reprinted 1963), 67, says of the rice and indigo planters, "There is no doubt that in per capita wealth and income, Low Country whites led all Americans." And Jackson Turner Main, *The Social Structure of Revolutionary America* (Princeton, 1965), 58–59, speaking of the same general group, says it was "unmistakably a society of great wealth." Main found the white residents of Charles Town much wealthier than those of Boston.

[58]*Statutes,* II, 662–76. All population figures in this section are taken from U.S. Bureau of the Census, *Historical Statistics of the United States, Colonial Times to 1957* (Washington, 1960), 756.

[59]*Statutes,* III, 82, 112–13.

[60]*Colonial South Carolina,* 226. Sirmans calculates the wealth per family as about £600 sterling, and I have taken the average family as consisting of six members.

[61]Manuscript Act 696. The sum of £51,195 11s 6d distributed evenly among 25,000 people results in taxation of £2 1s currency, or slightly less than 6s sterling.

[62]James Glen to Duke of Bedford, October 10, 1748, Sainsbury Transcripts, XXIII, 233.

[63]Manuscript Act 909. The white population in 1760 was about 36,740.

[64]Manuscript Act 990. The tax was for £70,326 7s 2d, and the white population was about 49,066. Marvin L. Michael Kay, "The Payment of Provincial and Local Taxes in North Carolina, 1748–1771," *William and Mary Quarterly,* 3d series, XXVI (1969), 239, calculates that the per capita annual tax collected in that less wealthy colony was 4s 7d sterling.

CHAPTER V

Selection and Appointment of the Public Treasurer

THE POWER TO APPOINT the public receiver or public treasurer was in dispute throughout the colonial period. The Commons House assumed that power from the very beginning, with the duty act of 1691 which created the office, and at one time it had statutory authority for its claim. After 1721 the Commons House could in the strictest sense only nominate a candidate, since the appointment was made by an ordinance which required the approval of the Council, and the governor was the one who actually commissioned the public treasurer. There were only a few major controversies between the two houses of the legislature, for only ten men were chosen to fill the office.

THE EARLY APPOINTMENTS

The appointment of Jonathan Amory as the first public receiver on September 26, 1691, seems to have occasioned no controversy. Amory served until his death in October 1699.[1] The governor and Council, who were authorized to make an interim appointment when an incumbent died, appointed George Logan to the office. Logan served until November 4, 1700, when the Dissenter-dominated Commons House insisted that Captain Thomas Smith (the second Landgrave, a Dissenter) be appointed. The Council reminded the Commons House that Parliament had recently passed a law prohibiting a member of Parliament from holding office and suggested that someone other than Smith, who was serving in the Commons House, be named. (Another member, Joseph Crosskeys, had been proposed for powder receiver.) The Commons House replied that it was of the opinion that an act of Parliament was not binding within the province until it was made of force by the Assembly. Then, turning the argument against those who advocated it, the Commons House, proposed that the members of the Council give up the offices which they held, because of the conflict of interest that was involved. (The Commons House denied that such a conflict could exist with the public receiver: "The Publick offices wch= ye Commons here have, a Power to Dispoose, of, Oblidges the Persons to Whome they are Given to serve the Interest of the Publick.") The counterargument apparently was enough to persuade the Council to abandon its position, for it shortly consented to let Smith take office, provided that he give bond for proper performance.[2]

Controlled by the Anglican faction after the elections of March 1703, the Commons House abruptly terminated Smith's tenure on April 24, 1703, claiming that he had made short entries of £622 5s ¼d in his accounts. The Commons House reinstated Logan, and he remained in office until his resignation on July 2, 1707.[3]

Logan resigned in the midst of the most significant early battle between the two houses of the Assembly for control of the office. In 1707 the Council objected to the continuation of Logan as public receiver, largely because he had become personally obnoxious to the governor and Council through his opposition to the Exclusion Act of 1704.[4] The Commons House maneuvered so adroitly in the struggle that, although Logan was not confirmed in office, the governor and Council not only accepted the second nomination of the Commons House but also agreed to approve an act which guaranteed it the right to nominate the public receiver in future years.

The sparring began on June 19, 1707, when the Commons House voted to continue Logan in office. The next day Governor Nathaniel Johnson sent a message in which he argued that the Council was allowed by the Carolina charter to appoint "any Judges Justices majestrates or other officers whatsoever wchin ye said Prouince at sea or Land . . .," and expressed surprise "That Instead of Leaving to us The True and absolute Lords and Proprietors Deputies The Right and freedom of Appointing Two Such Considerable Officers as ye Receiver and Comptroullr—you doe not Vouchsafe so much as To Take Our Aduice or Opinion Therein but nominate Them your Selues—Which being so Paliable and Incorachmt on there Lordspps Privillidges we Cannot by Noe means permit it."[5]

The Commons House agreed to the Council's demand that a joint committee be appointed to discuss the matter but denied the power of the Council over money matters, arguing by analogy that the House of Lords never interfered with money matters in England. The Council then tried to argue that the crown appointed the treasurer in England, so the governor and Council should have the same right in Carolina. The Commons House rejected this argument, saying that it alone should have the right to appoint the officer who was responsible for handling public moneys, lest they be misapplied. In response to the contention that the governor and Council had already approved a law giving the lower house the right to nominate the public receiver, the Council replied that the law had been passed by trickery. The Commons House answered that the law had been passed regularly by the three required readings and added wryly that "The Councell were not men of so Small Capasity to be so Trickt. . . ."[6]

The governor and Council were of the opinion that the only reason the Commons House wished to continue Logan in office was because he had sided with the Dissenters, who were then in control of that house. As Governor Johnson said in rather incoherent terms:

a Person so Justly obnoxious to the Govermt as Mr. Logan who hath made it his business to make Clubs, Parties & Factions & to be Principally Concernd in a notorious Riot, & Seconded with a Tumultous & most unreasonable Petition, & a Sedicious Association to Justify ye Same illegall & Extravigant Actions on purpose to Shelter ye Creminalls from Punishment by Those men & who upset on ye Account of Those ill Actions & affront & Turning agst. ye governmt. & for nothing Else is proposed to be Continued Receivr. . . .

Johnson proposed that Alexander Parris, who was not identified with either party in the struggle, be named to the position. Such action, he suggested, would stop the rumor circulated by an unnamed member of the Commons House that Johnson wanted to control the nomination so that he could receive bribes from candidates. He countered the rumor by telling the Commons House that it could ask Logan if Johnson had received any money from him for his appointment four years earlier, even though another member of the Commons House had offered him any amount he might ask for supporting that member's candidacy. If that candidate denied the truth of the charge, he added, "I Will Produce his Own Letter under his hand to Prove it. . . ." The governor concluded his message by indicating that he would hold the Assembly in session until it finished its business, including the paying of public debts, to let the people see who was responsible for the inaction on public affairs.[7]

The Commons House expressed what was probably only a mockingly ironic concern that Johnson was now rejecting "a Person whom your honr. hath always esteemd so well Quallified for That Trust That your honnr. did most Generally refuse all That was Proposed To you by Another hand, rather Then ye Publick Should be Deprived of ye Service of a man so fitt for That business. . . ." As to Parris' neutrality, the Commons House charged that it was the result of "Careless indifferency, or Rather a Slavish fear," suggesting that "he is a man of true worth & honnr. that When a Country is Divided boldly Espouseth ye Cause of That Party wch he belieues To have truth & justice on there Side. . . ." Johnson was reminded that he had once "very Publickly" called Parris such names as "Raskell Lyar &c. . . ." The Commons House concluded its verbal assault on Johnson by saying that the fact that someone had offered him a bribe proved that "all Persons should Rather aim to be Rewarded by ye Representation of there Country, for Serving it fairly & faith fully rather Then by Contracting with Gouernrs. Who haue Verry often, & may againe be Person Who rather Aim at in riching themselues then at ye. Public good wch. Cannot be Said of ye house of Commons."[8]

On June 27 Logan reported that Governor Johnson had "used very Sharpe & Reflecting Expressions agst him To mr. Edwd Weekley. . . ." Weekley was summoned to testify, and as a result the Commons House resolved not only that Logan was to be public receiver, but also that he was "not ye Occaision of ye Publick Differences," and that "ye Threatning words Spoken by ye Governr .. that he ye. Sd. Coll Logan Should Take Care of himselfe are Such as Concern ye Whole Assembly & Which They Look upon as Endeavouring to Ouerawe ye Assembly."[9]

When the governor and Council suggested that a third person be chosen jointly, the Commons House replied that to allow the Council any voice in the matter would be to give up the right in question. It proposed instead that if the governor would yield in the present issue, the question of who should choose the public receiver in the future would be put before the queen and parliament for resolution. The Council agreed, "Prouided you do not Choose mr. Logan or any Other Person undr Like Circumstances with him. . . ." That put the argument back where it started: The Commons House retorted that since Logan was its unanimous choice, agreeing on another candidate would be giving up the right of nomination.[10]

There might have been no resolution of the dilemma if Logan had not voluntarily chosen to resign in order to restore peace. The opposition of Governor Johnson and the Council to Logan seems to have been more personal than official. At any rate, they agreed to the appointment of George Smith to the office without opposition (Smith was Landgrave Thomas Smith's brother and he also had protested against the Exclusion Act) and even agreed to approve an act which seemed to guarantee to the Commons House the right to nominate the public receiver.[11] It was later argued, at least, by the Commons House that the act of 1707 gave it the right "to nominate a Publick Receiver, to put in place and displace all officers whatsoever, who receive any salary from the Public by order or appointment of the House of Commons."[12]

After the controversy of 1707, the public receivers seem to have been appointed to their office without serious difficulty until 1743. George Smith remained in office only a few months. He asked permission to resign because of the pressure of private business, and on November 14, 1707, Richard Beresford was chosen to replace him.[13] Beresford resigned on May 16, 1712. The Commons House offered Logan the position once more, but he declined, and it then appointed Alexander Parris on June 6, 1712.[14]

In 1721 during Parris's administration, royal government was established in South Carolina, and with it there was a settlement, at least in theory, of the issue of how the public receiver (now called the public treasurer) and all other civil officers who received a settled salary were to be chosen. The act of 1707 was repealed. Selection was to be by the joint action of the two houses of the Assembly, who were also to share the right to direct disbursements from the Public Treasury.[15] The Commons House never conceded, however, that the statute limited its right to nominate the public treasurer, arguing that the Council should routinely approve the nomination. Effectively, the law worked as the Commons House insisted that it should. The right of the Assembly to name the public treasurer independently of the governor was questioned even by the Board of Trade at one time, however. In 1756 the board directed Governor William Henry Lyttelton to secure repeal of the law and talked of disallowing the law of 1721 if repeal could not be secured. Nothing came of the effort.[16]

At one time Parris was limited to a three-year term by law, but the term was extended several times, and in 1716 an act specified that the public receiver should continue in office until removed by vote of the Commons House.[17] That situation did not arise until 1735, when Parris was removed for mishandling funds.[18] Four days later, on March 29, 1735, Gabriel Manigault received appointment without serious objection from the Council. That body merely pointed out that the appointment had not been made by a properly drawn ordinance, a defect which was quickly remedied. (Possibly the Commons House had quite forgotten how to appoint a public treasurer since Parris's original appointment in 1712.)[19] Manigault's greatest opposition came from within the Commons House itself; he came within one vote of losing the office to his rival, Othniel Beale.[20]

THE SCANDAL OF JACOB MOTTE'S APPOINTMENT

When Manigault submitted his resignation in March 1743, because he wished to devote full time to his private business, the stage was set for another major quarrel over the right of the governor and Council to participate in the selection of a successor, a quarrel which was further complicated by the intrusion of the officious Henry McCulloch into the debate. McCulloch held a special commission to investigate the collection of quitrents in South Carolina. He saw in the appointment of a new public treasurer an opportunity to increase the revenues collected through quitrents and presumed to suggest his own candidate for the position. Upon hearing of Manigault's intention to resign, McCulloch sent a letter to Lieutenant Governor William Bull, reminding him, as McCulloch said, of the King's desire that the offices of receiver general of the quitrents (held by George Saxby at that time) and public treasurer be united. The advantage to the collection of quitrents would be great, McCulloch urged, because provincial law required taxpayers to make sworn declarations of their property, but the law on quitrents could easily be evaded. McCulloch reasoned that the inquirers' tax lists could be used as the basis of a complete and accurate quitrent roll, which would ensure full payment of the rents.

Bull read the letter to the Council, which censured McCulloch for his "assuming and unbecoming" behavior. Bull maintained that he had received no instructions from the king on the matter, and the Council agreed that even if there had been an instruction, it would be unbecoming for McCulloch, an outsider, to remind Bull of his duties. Bull thereupon addressed a reply to McCulloch, asking sarcastically for his warrant for offering advice and saying that the lieutenant governor would confine himself to the advice of those persons appointed for that purpose by the king, that is, the Council.[21] The Council clearly intended to preserve its independence from pressures applied by royal officials from outside the province. Granted that McCulloch was officious and personally obnoxious, one cannot help but wonder what fears of being forced to pay full quitrents may have been masked by this assertion of a strict constitutional position.

Simultaneously with its rebuff to McCulloch, the Council was engaged in choosing its own candidate for the office of public treasurer. It unanimously agreed that one of its own members, Edmund Atkin, was well qualified. But Atkin noted that the law prohibited a councilor from holding the position and he did not wish to resign from the Council; further, he intended to leave soon on a trip to England. Casting about for another candidate, the Council agreed on Othniel Beale, who had come within one vote of being the Commons House's choice in 1735.[22]

A week later the Commons House selected Jacob Motte as its candidate. It did not even consider the name of Othniel Beale.[23] The ordinance of appointment then passed between the two bodies for the required three readings, with each house insisting on its original nominee. The Council on its third reading on April 9 reminded the Commons House that Manigault had tendered his resignation almost two weeks earlier. The Commons House was in no hurry to act, however, suggesting that since Manigault had not been given permission to resign there was really no need to consider the matter before the next meeting of the Assembly.[24]

After a brief interlude, the Commons House on April 26 retained Motte's name in its third reading of the ordinance.[25] A conference committee produced no agreement. The Commons House was beginning to search for a compromise candidate and was considering William Cattell, Jr., when it was astounded to learn that the Council had agreed to accept Motte.[26] Since the Council had seemed as adamant about maintaining its prerogatives as had the Commons House, something remarkable had evidently happened to cause it to change its mind. The possibility of scandal and severe embarrassment to the Commons House unfolded when it was learned a few days later that there had been a bargain to persuade Beale to withdraw. The Commons House immediately appointed a committee to investigate the rumors.[27]

The affair came out into the open on May 3, when Motte himself testified before the Commons House. He reported that after a second conference committee had failed to resolve the dispute between the two houses, it had been proposed that the governor be asked to name the public treasurer. But because the Commons House had already adjourned for the day, no message was sent. In the meantime several members of the Commons House had expressed the fear that the action might create a precedent and that the governor would always settle disputes by siding with the Council. Motte therefore had determined to treat with Beale directly, after a few attempts to deal through a third party had failed. According to the testimony, Motte proposed to Beale that Beale should become his surety on his bond and pay half the clerk's wages in exchange for half the profits of the office for three or four years. Motte stoutly maintained that no harm had been done to anyone and that he had acted from the purest of motives, that of preventing damage to the prestige of the Commons House.[28]

By present-day standards, Motte's conduct would have been reprehensible, but in eighteenth-century politics, the buying and selling of offices was common, for offices were often regarded as a form of personal estate. The office of public treasurer of South Carolina was not technically the vested property of its holder, for the Assembly could remove the holder without compensating him for his loss, but it was valuable as a source of income. (The last public treasurer, Henry Peronneau, seems to have considered the office as property, for he sought compensation from the British government when he lost it to the revolutionary regime.) The Commons House was hardly worried about the moral aspects of the affair but rather about the political consequences. Satisfied that its power to name the public treasurer had been enhanced rather than jeopardized, the Commons House proceeded to confirm Motte in the office.[29] Lieutenant Governor Bull signed the ordinance on May 6, and the crisis was over.[30]

APPOINTMENT OF THE JOINT PUBLIC TREASURERS

The next, and last, occasion for dispute over appointment of a public treasurer occurred upon Motte's death on June 17, 1770, after twenty-seven years in the office. Henry Peronneau had been Motte's assistant since May 1767[31] and had really transacted all the business of the office because of Motte's poor health. Accordingly, he felt entitled to the office when it fell vacant. But Motte's death occurred in the midst of the famous "Wilkes fund controversy," and the appointment of a public treasurer momentarily became a political football as the Commons House and the Council found a new way to express their hostilities toward each other over the Wilkes affair.[32] Benjamin Dart, a member of the Commons House who was identified with the patriotic faction, submitted a petition for the office in competition with Peronneau. The Council suggested that the two might become joint public treasurers, but the Commons House initially insisted on Dart's appointment alone, probably to reward him for his faithful support in recent debates. Both houses maintained their positions on a second reading of the ordinance of appointment, and partially because of the deadlock Lieutenant Governor William Bull prorogued the Assembly for several months.[33]

Shortly after reconvening, the Commons House rather surprisingly not only accepted the idea of joint public treasurers but even agreed to let Peronneau's name precede that of Dart in the ordinance of appointment.[34] Jack P. Greene concludes that the arrangement was a compromise. Each faction placed a candidate in office. The penalty clause required by the royal authorities to prevent disbursements by the Commons House alone, as in the Wilkes case, was not put in the appointing ordinance but in the bonds posted by the two men.[35] Peronneau and Dart continued in office until April 9, 1776, when the revolutionary Provincial Congress revoked their commissions and turned over control of the Public Treasury to three commissioners.[36]

FACTORS IN SELECTION

It is apparent that one of the prime qualifications of a candidate for the office of public treasurer was acceptability to a political grouping that usually involved control of the Commons House. Jonathan Amory may have owed his appointment to his friendship with Seth Sothell, the troublesome proprietor who took over the government of South Carolina in 1690 because of his seniority. Eugene Sirmans credits Sothell with getting the duty act of 1691 passed, and it seems reasonable that the first public receiver should have been associated with the Sothell faction. But Amory soon became disenchanted with Sothell, as did nearly everyone, and joined with the group of moderates who followed the leadership of Joseph Blake.[37]

Since Logan was made public receiver on an interim basis by
Governor Blake and the Council at a time when there was little
divisiveness in the province,[38] no special significance can be attached to his selection. Since he was removed from office as soon
as the Dissenters came to control the Commons House and was
returned to office when the Anglicans regained power, it seems
certain, however that Logan was originally on the Anglican side in
the disputes that broke out upon Blake's death in 1700. Subsequently, he became a favorite of the Commons House and
anathema to the Council because of his opposition to the Exclusion Act.

Logan's example shows how a shift in a man's political stance
might influence his standing with the Common House. Often it
was a change within that body itself which would work a change in
the man's standing. The most obvious examples are those already
cited: a faction's coming to power was enough to secure the re-
moval of a public receiver and his replacement by that faction's
candidate.

A change in the political situation, or the mere passage of
time, might make a man more acceptable. The Commons House
flatly refused to consider Parris for office in 1707 but chose him
routinely only five years later. The difference was, of course, that
in 1707 Parris was the candidate sponsored by the Council, and in
1712 he was the Commons House's free choice. By way of con-
trast, in 1735 when there was no dispute over the right to name
the public treasurer, the Commons House came within one vote
of naming Othniel Beale to the position. In 1743, simply because
the Council supported Beale, the Commons House would not
even consider his candidacy.

From 1700 to about 1712 political divisions tended to reflect
religious differences. The Council was always the Anglican
Church party, the Commons House was usually controlled by
Dissenters, and the public receiver was always a Dissenter during
those years, if Logan's conversion is counted. Governor Charles
Craven, who took office in March 1712, indicated that Dissenters
would not be deprived of their privileges despite the official status
of the Church of England, and after 1712 religious issues were not

seriously divisive. Beginning in 1735 the office of public treasurer was always held by men whose French Huguenot ancestors had been hated by Dissenters even more than by Anglicans and who had had even their right to vote challenged in the 1690s.[39] Now the earlier hostilities had been forgotten, and Manigault, Motte, and Peronneau were entrusted with the keys of the public treasury.

Perhaps the chief reason that the public treasurer was usually acceptable to the Commons House is that he was nearly always a Commons House man. In fact, nearly all were serving in that house at the time they were elected to office (before 1721 they could continue their membership in the Assembly while they held the office, there being no law to prohibit it). Peronneau was the only public treasurer who did not have a career in the Commons House, and he was not that body's candidate. The two men who were considered by the Commons House but not finally selected for public treasurer—Othniel Beale and William Cattell, Jr.— were also members. Of the Public Treasurers who were Commons House members, all were important enough to be listed by Jack P. Greene as leaders, and all except Motte served at least part of the time in the "first rank" of leadership. Three were so highly placed that they were elected speaker: Amory was twice chosen while he was public receiver, and Thomas Smith and Logan were chosen after they had left the Treasury.[40]

The men who were public treasurers tended to be active outside the Commons House as well, holding numerous other offices. When Parris died in 1736 the newspaper reported that "He had the Honour to be in all publick Offices in this Government, Civil and Military, both of Honour and Profit, in all of which he never had regard to his private Interest."[41] The statement is not literally true. He apparently was very much influenced by private interest in his treasury operations, and he did not hold anything like all the different offices the province had to offer. He did occupy many of them. He was a justice of the peace, probably throughout his adult life. In 1700 he was "High Sherife of Berkly County." He served as powder receiver and captain of the fort from 1701 to 1703, during which time he was also a member of the Council, presumably as a proprietor's deputy. He advanced from one rank to another in the militia, being referred to as captain early in 1700, major in 1706, and colonel by 1712. As colonel of the militia, he was particularly instrumental in the overthrow of the proprietary government in 1719. He was on the commission which supervised the Free School in Charles Town beginning in 1712, and he was also a commissioner for buying "Bucketts Ladder and ffirehooks ffor the Suppressing of ffires in Charles Town" in 1706. After 1721 he was an assistant judge of the Supreme and General Court.[42]

Parris doubtless held other offices (he had a reputation for being a real politician), but no attempt was made by the author to find every biographical fact about each public treasurer. It appears that Gabriel Manigault, although not regarded as a politician, held an even wider variety of offices. He was a justice of the peace from 1732 until at least 1777 and vestryman of St. Philip's parish 1732–37 and 1765–79. He served on numerous commissions: finishing St. Philip's Church building, in the late 1730s; church establishment, from 1738 until at least 1775; building St. Michael's Church, in the 1750s; fortifications, 1753–56 and 1767–68; streets, 1750 and 1764–75; the Free School in Charles Town, probably from 1742 to 1775 (he was vice president after 1760); and workhouse and markets, 1744–45. He was cashier to the directors of the Cherokee trade, 1762–65, and treasurer to the commissioners of the silk manufacture from 1766 until at least 1778. He was twice recommended for appointment to the Council by Lieutenant Governor Bull, but neither time did the Board of Trade appoint any of the persons recommended by Bull.[43] Not every public treasurer could match the achievements in public service of Parris and Manigault, but each was generally very active in politics.

Nearly every public treasurer was a merchant. Only Thomas Smith is identified as a planter, although several others had fairly large landholdings. Parris owned several thousand acres, and if Manigault had not preferred to call himself a merchant (he was perhaps the wealthiest in the province) he could have qualified as a planter more important than most who so styled themselves. It might be argued that mercantile experience would have better qualified a man for the position than planting, but it is doubtful. The wretched bookkeeping and money-handling practices of Parris and Motte, both merchants, suggest that any competent person—planter, merchant, or whatever—could have done a better job. Probably the Commons House did not consciously choose merchants because of their occupations. Merchants came to dominate the House, and by choosing its own members, as it nearly always did, the Commons House stood a good chance of choosing a merchant. Such a practice ensured that Berkeley County or its parishes dominated the treasury, since merchants seldom worked out of Beaufort or George Town.[44]

It is difficult to generalize about age as a factor in selection, because the life spans of only half the officers are known. Of those five, three were under forty when appointed, and Gabriel Manigault was only thirty-one. It would appear, then, that young men probably had an advantage. It is curious, however, that the men who were older when appointed served the longest terms of all. Motte was forty-three and served until he was seventy; Parris was fifty-one and served until he was almost seventy-five. As a group, the public treasurers were remarkably long-lived. Thomas Smith lived to be seventy-four, and Manigault died at the age of seventy-seven.[45]

From the preceding information it is possible to sketch a composite portrait of a public treasurer. One could assume that a young Charles Town merchant who was a Dissenter or a Huguenot, had already been active in politics, and had advanced to important committee assignments in the Commons House would be a good contender for the appointment. If, in addition, he was known to be perfectly willing to follow the dictates of the Commons House and to ignore the claims to prerogative power asserted by the governor and Council, he would almost certainly be seriously considered. He might find competition from someone very much like himself, but if he were the man of the Commons House, it would not matter how the Council was disposed toward him. He would almost certainly be the next public treasurer.

NOTES

[1]*Statutes*, II, 65; A.S. Salley, "Abstracts from the Records of the Court of Ordinary of the Province of South Carolina, 1700–1712," *South Carolina Historical and Genealogical Magazine*, XII (1911), 72.

[2]Commons House Journal, November 1–2, 4, 1700, *JCH, 1700*, 6–10. The act is not extant, but it is likely that the formal appointment was made in the duty act of November 16, 1700. *Statutes*, II, 162.

[3]Commons House Journal, April 24, 1703, *JCH, 1703*, 68; July 2, 1707, *Journal of the Commons House of Assembly of South Carolina, June 5, 1707–July 19, 1707*, ed. A.S. Salley (Columbia, 1940), 72–73; *Statutes*, II, 204; Sirmans, *Colonial South Carolina*, 87.

[4]The act had required that all members of the Commons House either be communicants of the Church of England or take the oath of conformity. It was repealed in 1706. *Statutes*, II, 232–35, 281.

[5]Commons House Journal, June 19–20, 1707, *JCH, 1707*, 42, 45.

[6]Commons House Journal, June 20, 1707, ibid., 46–50.

[7]Commons House Journal, June 25, 1707, ibid., 58–59.

[8]Commons House Journal, June 25, 1707, ibid., 61–62.

[9]Commons House Journal, June 27, 1707, ibid., 66.

[10]Commons House Journal, June 27, 1707, ibid., 67–69.

[11]Commons House Journal, July 2–3, 5, 1707, ibid., 72–74, 83; *Statutes*, II, 305. The act declaring the right of the Commons House to nominate is not extant, but the title is given in *Statutes*, II, 299.

[12]Commons House Journal, June 30, 1716, V, 147.

[13]Commons House Journal, November 14, 1707, *JCH, 1707*, 42–43.

[14]Commons House Journal, June 6, 1712, IV, 81.

[15]*Statutes*, III, 148–49.

[16]"South Carolina's Colonial Constitution: Two Proposals for Reform," ed. Jack P. Greene, *South Carolina Historical Magazine*, LXII (1961), 81.

[17]*Statutes*, II, 656.

[18]See Chapter II.

[19]Commons House Journal, March 28, 29, 1735, *JCH, 1734–1735*, 138, 153, 155, 157–58.

[20]Commons House Journal, March 25, 1735, ibid., 134.

[21]Council Journal, March 23–24, 1742/3, X, 74–75, 83–84; Henry McCulloch to Board of Trade, March 25, 1743, Sainsbury Transcripts, XXI, 142–46. Charles G. Sellers, Jr., "Private Profits and British Colonial Policy: The Speculations of Henry McCulloch," *William and Mary Quarterly*, 3d series, VIII (1951), 535–51, gives insights into McCulloch's character.

[22]Upper House Journal, March 23–24, 1742/3, CJ, IX, 2d pagination, 56–57.

[23]Commons House Journal, March 31, 1743, *JCH, 1742–1744*, 349.

[24]Commons House Journal, April 9, 1743, ibid., 382.

[25]Commons House Journal, April 26, 1743, ibid., 385.

[26]Commons House Journal, April 29, 1743, ibid., 414.

[27]Commons House Journal, April 30, 1743, ibid., 414–15.

[28]Commons House Journal, May 3, 1743, ibid., 422–23.

[29]Commons House Journal, May 3, 1743, ibid., 423.

[30]Council Journal, May 6, 7, 1743, X, 200, 210. It appears from Gabriel Man-

igault's posting of bond for Motte that the bargain with Beale was not actually consummated.

[31]Commons House Journal, May 22, 1767, xxxvii, Part One, 2d pagination, 410.

[32]See Chapter VI.

[33]Commons House Journal, August 23, 29–30, September 6–8, 1770, xxxviii, Part Two, 422–23, 430, 441, 449–50, 453–56.

[34]Commons House Journal, February 7, 1771, ibid., Part Three, 477–78.

[35]"Bridge to Revolution: The Wilkes Fund Controversy in South Carolina," *Journal of Southern History*, xxix (1963), 32. Robert M. Weir, *"A Most Important Epocha": The Coming of the Revolution in South Carolina* (Columbia, 1970), 39–50, gives a briefer account. Greene has also edited *The Nature of Colony Constitutions: Two Pamphlets on the Wilkes Fund Controversy in South Carolina* (Columbia, 1970).

[36]*Statutes*, iv, 342–43.

[37]*Colonial South Carolina*, 50–52.

[38]Ibid., 70.

[39]Ibid., 61–62.

[40]Greene, *Quest for Power*, 459–60.

[41]*South-Carolina Gazette*, March 13, 1735/6.

[42]Ibid., June 15, 1734; Commons House Journal, October 30, 1700, *JCH, 1700*, 3; August 28, 1701, *JCH, August 1701*, 31; January 15, 1701/2, *JCH, 1702*, 4; June 6, 1712, iv, 81; March 8, 13, 1705/6, *JCH, 1706*, 15, 25; A.S. Salley, "Abstracts from the Records of the Court of Ordinary of the Province of South Carolina, 1692–1700," *South Carolina Historical and Genealogical Magazine*, x (1909), 89; *Statutes*, ii, 342; Smith, *South Carolina as a Royal Province*, 123; Ramsay, *History of South Carolina*, i, 81.

[43]Maurice A. Crouse, The Manigault Family of South Carolina, 1685–1783 (Ph.D. dissertation, Northwestern University, 1964), Chapter XI.

[44]A.S. Salley, "Abstracts from the Records of the Court of Ordinary of the Province of South Carolina, 1700–1712,"*South Carolina Historical and Genealogical Magazine*, xii (1911), 72; *Statutes*, ii, 204, 305; Sirmans, *Colonial South Carolina*, 105, 110, 146, 247n, 353.

[45]"Publications Received," *South Carolina Historical and Genealogical Magazine*, ii (1901), 304; "The Register of Christ Church Parish," ed. Mabel L. Webber, ibid., xxi (1920), 105; "Colonel Alexander Parris, and Parris Island," comp. Mabel L. Webber, ibid., xxvi (1925), 144; Greene, *Quest for Power*, 524 (index entry for Thomas Smith); *Dictionary of American Biography*, ed. Allen Johnson and Dumas Malone (20 vols.; New York, 1928–1936), xii, 234.

CHAPTER VI

Supervision and Control

THERE COULD BE BUT FEW CONTROVERSIES over the appointment of a public treasurer because of the relatively few times the office became vacant, especially after 1712. But over such matters as control of expenditures from the Treasury and the drafting of money bills, opportunities for disagreement between the Commons House and the Council were frequent. The Commons House, always viewing the House of Commons in Parliament as its model, maintained that it alone was responsible for money matters, but the instructions given to the governors usually specified that they had the right to order payments from the Treasury with the consent of the Council, or at least that the Council was to share equally with the Commons House in determining money matters.[1] Here was the cause of many a dispute. The Commons House won most of the important battles over finance in the early years but was not able to maintain the exclusive control over the Public Treasury which it claimed, and which it in fact exercised from about 1755 to 1770. The colonial period ended with the Commons House on one side and the governor and Council on the other deadlocked over the issue of control.

INDIRECT TACTICS OF CONTROL

The Commons House used many tactics in its struggle to control finances. Most involved direct confrontation with the Council and governor, but there were two ways by which the Commons House sought to outflank its opponents. By appointing various commissions to supervise governmental matters and by authorizing them to draw upon the Public Treasury, the Commons House intruded upon what was meant by the authorities to be the preserve of the governor. Typical of this approach was the appointment of the commissioners of fortifications, to whose functions both Governor Glen and the Board of Trade voiced ineffectual objections.[2] The committee could issue orders for payment from the Treasury from the funds allotted to fortifications without any further approval by anyone.[3] Though irritated, Governor Glen had to put up with the commissioners, and in an understandable fit of pique he once appointed several of his severest critics on the matter of fortifications to the commission.[4]

Other agencies which could draw upon the Treasury were the vestries of the parishes; the church establishment commission (the lay commission begun in 1706 to oversee the church's operations); the commissary-general; the commissioners for building both the old and the new state houses; the commissioners for building church buildings in the parishes of St. Andrew and Prince George, Winyaw; the inspectors of flax, linen, and thread; and the commissioners for building an addition to the "halfe moon," an early part of the fortifications.[5]

Perhaps the cleverest of the tactics devised by the Commons House was "borrowing" funds from the public treasurer. Since the funds were technically not appropriated but only "borrowed," the Commons House did not ask for the approval of the Council or the governor. The "repaying" of the "loan" would occur when the Commons House inserted the amount in the schedule of governmental charges attached to the annual tax bill. Because the Council had by 1748 lost its power to amend money bills and because the governor had no item veto, the only way to disapprove of the "borrowing" was for them to reject the entire tax bill. Ordinarily, then, the Commons House was allowed to disburse funds in this way without effective challenge. Lieutenant Governor Bull did not even officially protest the "borrowing" of £600 to pay for the expenses of South Carolina's delegates to the Stamp Act Congress.[6] But as Jack P. Greene has pointed out, the exercise of this power provided the "bridge to revolution" in South Carolina when the province chose in 1769 to borrow for a gift to

John Wilkes, an enemy of the king. In the midst of that controversy, so simple a matter as the ordering of the payment of £300 to the commissioners of the silk manufacture was enough to precipitate a governmental crisis.[7]

THE FUNDAMENTAL ISSUE

The fundamental issue between the two houses was the dispute over the authority to direct payment from the Public Treasury. Typical of many such controversies was the debate in 1737 over Lieutenant Governor Thomas Broughton's order that £1,650 be paid to several officials out of the township fund for various fees connected with granting land to incoming poor Protestant settlers. The Commons House protested that the act which created the fund allowed disbursements only for tools, provisions, and other necessities, and ordered the public treasurer not to pay the sums.[8] Both sides had some precedent for their arguments. The act of 1735 did read as the Commons House said, but an earlier statute of 1731, which had not been entirely superseded, had allowed payment for expenses of surveying and laying out lands in the new townships.[9]

A few months later the Council summoned the public treasurer, Gabriel Manigault, and reminded him that the lieutenant governor, with the advice of the Council, had ordered payment. Caught between both bodies, Manigault refused to commit himself to a constitutional squabble. He tactfully assured the Council that all debts would be discharged insofar as possible as soon as money came into his hands from the sinking and all prior debts had been paid.[10]

The fees were still unpaid five months later, when Broughton demanded to know the reasons for the order of the Commons House.[11] After Broughton's death, Council President James Kinloch delivered an ultimatum to the Commons House: the Council would refuse its assent to any orders on the township fund sent up by the Commons House until the fees had been paid. At the same time the Council ordered Manigault not to pay any orders not approved by the Council.[12] The controversy was finally compromised in March 1737/8, when it was agreed that the ban on payment of orders not having the Council's approval would be lifted, and that all orders drawn by Broughton, Kinloch, and the Council would be paid.[13] Neither group had won its point.

EXAMINING THE PUBLIC TREASURER'S BOOKS

If Manigault had paid the lieutenant governor's order without the approval of the Commons House, that body probably would have refused to approve his accounts, and he would have been personally liable for replacing the amount in the Treasury. It was largely through the power to approve or disallow the public treasurer's accounts that the Commons House made that officer ultimately responsible only to itself. Exactly how early the Commons House used this kind of control has not been ascertained, but there was a case as early at 1711 where an order by the governor which had not been approved by the Commons House was not allowed.[14]

The duty act of 1691 which created the Public Treasury specified that the public receiver's accounts were to be sent to the parliament (the South Carolina, not the British, legislature), suggesting that the lower house would not monopolize control. But thereafter the Commons House lost few opportunities to insist that it alone had the right to inspect the accounts. In 1701 there occurred the first significant debate on the matter. When the Council called for the public receiver's accounts, the Commons House resolved that "The Publick Receiver is Accountable to the Commons only." The Council made the point that it could hardly legislate intelligently if it did not know the state of the Treasury, and the Commons House then relented its position to allow the Council to see the accounts, but "only for their Perusiall." When the Council protested its not being able to see the books at will, the Commons House replied that councilors "may and ought to See ye Publick Receivers accots when and as often as you please."[15] The Commons House's first attempt to deny the Council access to the public treasurer's records thus resulted in a complete backing down.

Until 1755 the Council participated fairly actively in the examination of the public treasurer's accounts. In 1739, however, encouraged by its success in battles with the Council on other points, the Commons House tried to shut out the Council from the committee to audit the public treasurer's accounts. The committee had always been a joint committee, with members from the Commons House predominating. Now the Commons House proposed that its own committee examine and approve the accounts before they were turned over to a committee of the Council. The Council asked, "For to what Purpose shall the other House, in such Case, examine them at all, afterwards?" At the first session of the Assembly the Council did not have its way, but at the second session the Commons House agreed to invite members of the Council to sit with its committee.[16] Finally in 1755, when the Commons House was seeking to deny the Council any access to the documents used in drafting the tax acts, the Commons House determined that the Council should not have any role in approving financial accounts. Although the resolution did not specifically mention the public treasurer's books, it appears that the Council's examination of them ceased at that time. The records contain many statements of approval of the accounts between the dates of May 26, 1736, and May 11, 1754, all signed by the governor, president of the Council, and speaker of the Commons House, but there are none after 1754.[17]

The purpose of the examination of the Treasury books was to ensure that no funds were disbursed contrary to law and that the funds were properly accounted for. At various times the Commons House took its power of examination seriously, but at others the examination was extremely lax, even careless. At first the accounts were examined according to no schedule at all, only when the Commons House saw fit.[18] Somewhat later a committee of the Commons House was appointed and instructed to examine the books every two months, or at more frequent intervals if the committee found it necessary.[19] Still later the interval was established at three months.[20] There is little to indicate that the books were actually examined so frequently, and for the period for which the Treasury records are extant, mostly after 1735, the examination was usually made no more often than annually. In

1755 the Commons House ordered that the public treasurer settle his accounts on January 1 of each year so that he could have his books ready for examination by the auditing committee.[21] The examination usually proceeded along with the preparation of the annual tax bill so that any balances in the various funds could be applied toward reducing the amount of taxation, if desired by the Assembly.

The thoroughness of the examination is doubtful, especially for the latter period of Parris's administration as public treasurer. In 1733 the committee reported examining accounts as far back as 1726, an indication that the accounts had not been examined at all for some time (it is likely that the disruptions during the controversy over paper money in the late 1720s had prevented examination). Although a few discrepancies were found, some of them apparently of a major order, the accounts were signed without question by the speaker.[22] It was not until March 1734/5 that a special examination of the records revealed wholesale disregard of law and accounting procedures on the part of Parris.[23]

AUDITING THE ACCOUNTS OF PUBLIC CREDITORS

Most of the serious struggles between Commons House and Council centered around the passage of taxation measures. The way in which tax bills were framed after 1733 gave the Commons House a considerable advantage. The political and economic chaos of the years prior to 1731 had resulted in the accumulation of a large public debt because no tax bill had been passed since 1727. An act of 1731 listed the debts and provided for their payment from various funds that would be made available from taxes and duties. The tax act of 1733 used the same procedure for paying the debts of the previous year.[24] Thereafter the province never attempted to anticipate expenses but chose rather to work "on credit," requiring public creditors to submit accounts of their claims and then providing for their payment by legislation. This system allowed little room for independent spending by the governor or the Council; if they chose to order disbursement from the Treasury, they were expected to submit their accounts, just

like private creditors, for the consideration of the Commons
House. Governor Glen in particular did not like this control. He
wrangled with the Commons House in 1752 over the requirement
that he furnish papers, including financial accounts, relating to
Indian affairs. Glen called the Commons House's request "unprecedented & unparliamentary" and said that he would furnish
no papers at all until he had finished action on the matters under
consideration.[25] Governor Glen ran afoul of the Commons House
again in 1754, whereupon the Commons House declared that it
would not provide for any accounts that were not subjected to the
usual examination by its committee.[26]

The auditing of the accounts of creditors of the government
to ascertain how much should be raised by the tax was one of the
preliminary steps to framing a tax bill. Until about 1736 or 1737
the Council appears to have had active members on the auditing
committee. But in 1737 the Commons House refused to confer
on the accounts with the Council. Although the Council protested, it did eventually consent to a tax bill based on accounts
which had not been jointly approved, and in succeeding years the
practice of having the Commons House alone frame the estimate
of government charges became standard.[27]

From that time until 1755 the Council still viewed the accounts, but only after they had been scrutinized by the Commons
House and inserted in the estimate for the tax bill. In 1755, during the controversy over the payment of the salary and expenses
of the colonial agent in England, the Commons House refused
even that courtesy, maintaining that the practice of the British
Parliament afforded no precedent for it. It passed a resolution
stating that "no Account Petition or other Paper that shall be
presented to or laid before this House of for or concerning any
Claim or demand whatever for any matter or thing done or to be
done for the service of the Public shall be sent to the Council for
their inspection."[28]

The Council acquiesced in 1755 because of the need for
money to help fight the French and Indian War. In 1756, however, the Council asked for accounts and refused to legislate on
the tax bill until it received them. The Commons House could not
deny that accounts had been sent to the Council in previous years,

but it maintained that the Council had always received them as a matter of privilege and not of right. When Governor Glen suggested that the Council's inspection of the accounts was after all a small matter, the Commons House objected that, on the contrary, the dispute concerned the "most valuable Rights & Liberties" of the people.[29]

Governor Glen was eager to get a tax bill passed so that he could proceed with his defense plans and finally urged the Council to pass it without seeing the accounts, arguing that the Council was not really abandoning its rights but merely postponing the controversy, in the interest of the public welfare, until a more convenient time. The bill was finally passed in June 1756, after the arrival of Governor Lyttelton. When it looked as if the entire scenario might be replayed, Lyttelton prevailed upon the Council to accept the advice which Glen had given.[30] That ended the controversy, and the Commons House had won its point for all time.

AMENDING MONEY BILLS

Although after 1756 the Council did not have the power to examine the accounts of public creditors, it still had the power of considering tax legislation and could, if it desired, refuse to approve a bill.[31] By a series of struggles, the Council gradually lost its ability to amend a money bill, but its ultimate control over the passage or rejection of a bill remained in contention until the end of the colonial period. In fact, this controversy helped to hasten the end of the colonial period—it led rather directly into revolution in South Carolina.

The process started in 1725 when the Commons House deleted the Council's amendments from the tax bill, and the Council restored them on the third and final reading. Each house was accused by the other of violating parliamentary procedure, the Commons House for deleting the amendments without conferring with the Council, and the Council for amending a bill when it could not be reconsidered by the Commons House.[32] After a prorogation, the controversy was reopened with the Council in-

sisting on its right to share in legislating money bills by virtue of
Governor Nicholson's thirty-fifth instruction and the Commons
House appealing to the precedent of the British Constitution,
insisting that only the elected representatives of the people could
legislate on those matters. Because of the pressing need for
money, the Council gave way, but not without bitterly protesting
that the Commons House was usurping its prerogatives.[33]

For several years thereafter the Commons House swung between two positions, at times denying that the Council could
amend and at others allowing that body to make amendments to
money bills. In 1735 and 1739 there occurred struggles which led
to the elimination of the Council from the framing of money bills.
The controversy originated over the refusal of the Commons
House to pay a salary to the unpopular Chief Justice Robert
Wright. When the Council added the sum of £2,100 to the estimate to cover the salary, the Commons House erupted in
eloquent protest. Employing the language of Charles Pinckney, it
argued that the House of Commons in England had sole right
and power over money, that the Commons House of Assembly of
South Carolina had the same right, and that therefore "after the
Estimate is closed, and added to any Tax Bill, that no Additions
can or ought to be made thereto, by any other Estate or power
whatsoever, but by and in the Commons House of Assembly."[34]
The Council appealed but in vain to the authority of Nicholson's
thirty-fifth instruction; it had to accept a tax bill which did not
provide for Wright's salary.[35] Wright was finally given, in 1736,
£700 in full settlement of his claims.[36]

The controversy was resolved in a similar dispute in 1739. In
April of that year the Council sought to amend two money bills,
only to have the amendments rejected by the Commons House as
unparliamentary. A debate similar in most respects to that of 1735
then ensued.[37] The Commons House was adamant in its rejection
of the Council's contention that Governor Nicholson's instruction
authorized the Council to share in legislation on money matters:
"A Power to abrogate old Laws or impose new ones upon the
People, without their Consent, is a Prerogative that the Crown
never exercised or assumed to itself over any Part of the

Realm. . . . The Power of raising and levying of Money is of the many Privileges we enjoy; the most essential; and upon which all the rest seem to depend. If that Corner Stone is once removed, the Superstructure of Course will fall to the Ground."[38]

The Assembly adjourned without voting a tax bill, and on the advice of the Council, Lieutenant Governor Bull dissolved the Assembly and called for new elections.[39] The situation had not changed materially. The Council refused even to consider a tax bill until it had had the privilege of sitting with a committee of the Commons House to evaluate the accounts, a renewal of the controversy of 1737.[40] After considerable debate, the two houses agreed upon a *modus vivendi* which was regarded as temporary by both houses at the time but which solidified into standing practice for almost ten years. The agreement applied to all bills, but the seventh paragraph dealt specifically with money bills. It provided that if the Council wished to propose amendments to a money bill, a schedule of amendments should be sent to the Commons House along with the original bill. If the Commons House saw fit to approve them, the changes would be added to the bill and the amended bill then sent back to the Council for final approval.[41] The agreement does not seem to have been recognized by the Commons House for the great victory that it was. Although it gave the Commons House the right of vetoing any changes made by the Council, the lower house regarded it with some suspicion, asserting that the compromise did not affect its "sole Right of introducing, framing, altering and amending subsidy Bills. . . ." For its part, the Council maintained that it was not giving up its "just Claim . . . to the amending Money Bills. . . ."[42] But the Council was deluding itself. It might suggest amendments, but it could not compel them. The final word would rest in the Commons House.

Under this arrangement the Commons House sometimes accepted Council amendments and sometimes rejected them. In 1748 it agreed to accept first three, then seven of fourteen amendments proposed by the Council to the tax bill of that year. However, it then resolved "that no Agreement should at any Time be made with the Council to countenance or warrant their sending any Schedule of Amendments at any Time to the Tax Bill or Estimate or any Subsidy Bill."[43] The Council seems thereafter to have been effectively prevented from even suggesting amendments.

REJECTION OF MONEY BILLS

Even if the Council could not amend, it could still refuse to pass a money bill. In 1764 the Commons House deleted from the schedule for the annual tax the amount of £7,000 which was to have covered an arrears of two years in the salary of Governor Thomas Boone, who had only recently departed the province after the bitterly fought Gadsden election controversy.[44] Protesting that the deletion was contrary to the king's instructions and an affront to Boone, the Council requested restoration of the amount.[45] The Commons House, of course, disagreed with the proposed amendment, explaining in mock surprise that it knew of no power of the Council to provide anything, since the appropriation of funds was a function of the Commons House. Furthermore, the sum asked for was not a salary but a gratuity from the people, and Governor Boone, the Commons House said, clearly did not deserve it.[46] The Council refused to accept the tax bill as it stood, and it was more than a month before Lieutenant Governor Bull could use his influence to persuade the Council to accept the bill without provision for the salary.[47] That sum was not paid until 1766, when the new governor, Lord Charles Greville Montagu, presented an additional instruction which specifically required that South Carolina provide for Boone. Even then, the Commons House avoided the appearance of bowing to instructions by providing the salary ostensibly as a demonstration of gratitude for the repeal of the Stamp Act.[48]

Perhaps the greatest crisis occasioned by the disputes over control of finances was the "Wilkes fund controversy."[49] On December 8, 1769, the Commons House directed the public treasurer to pay £10,500 "to certain Gentlemen, who are to remit the same to great Britain, for the Support of the just and Constitutional Rights and Liberties of the People of Great Britain and

America." The Commons House agreed to reimburse the Public Treasurer for the amount which was being "borrowed."[50]

The vagueness of the entry in the journal of the Commons House was a true indication of the deviousness it so poorly concealed. The "certain Gentlemen" were the speaker and six other members of the Commons House, who wrote the next day to the Supporters of the Bill of Rights—the organization which supported John Wilkes—in London, informing the organization of the gift which had been voted.[51] Wilkes was noted for his attack upon the king in the forty-fifth number of his *North Briton,* his several expulsions from the House of Commons, and his immoral private life. The Commons House of Assembly of South Carolina did not condone his personal affairs but looked on its gift to the society as a blow for freedom.[52]

The course that the Commons House had set was a dangerous one. Lieutenant Governor Bull had frequently condoned resolutions and actions that might be deemed derogatory of royal authority, but there were limits beyond which he would not go. Allowing the Commons House to release its hostilities in relatively harmless ways was one thing; allowing it to mount a direct attack upon the king was another.

The Commons House wrote into the schedule of the public debt for 1769 the item of £10,500 advanced by the public treasurer to the "certain Gentlemen." The Council refused absolutely to permit its inclusion.[53] A committee of the Commons House reported that precedent for borrowing funds from the public treasurer was on the side of the lower house. In a daring move, designed to remove the influence of the Council altogether, the committee resurrected an earlier recommendation that an upper house of Assembly be appointed according to the original constitution and charter of Carolina. Any further action was stopped by Bull's proroguing the Assembly.[54]

As soon as the Assembly reconvened, the Commons House sought to reinforce its position by ordering the public treasurer to advance funds to defray the expenses of erecting a statue of William Pitt in honor of his services in getting the Stamp Act repealed. This was exactly the same procedure which had been used in the gift to Wilkes, and Bull hastened to prorogue the

Assembly once more.[55] When it met again, the Commons House only had time to renew its order for the payment before Bull prorogued the Assembly a third time.[56]

By August 16 Bull was in a position to do battle with the Commons House. He presented it with an additional instruction which had only recently arrived, forbidding the governor to give his assent to any bill for defraying expenses outside the province except on the king's requisition or to any bill granting money for any purposes other than that stated in its title. In future money bills there was to be added a clause which subjected the public treasurer or others entrusted with public moneys to the penalty of triple the amount involved for paying any sums illegally, and the official would be declared incapable thereafter of holding any office within the province.[57]

Bull and the Council made it clear that they intended to enforce the additional instruction, which would make it impossible in the future for the Commons House to dispose of public funds as it had done in the case of the gift to Wilkes, without the approval of either the Council or the governor. In the new tax bill the Council discovered that a charge for £10,500 "for a Strange and Extravagant purpose, was again intruded upon us" and unanimously rejected the tax bill.[58] Bull could not be tricked either. When the Commons House ordered the public treasurer to pay him £7 to provide necessary articles for each poor Irish Protestant who had arrived in the province recently, Bull replied that the proposal was "very agreeable" to him, but he regretted that it was provided on the sole authority of an order of the Commons House rather than by an ordinance of the Assembly, "which by the Royal Instruction, is to be my rule in issuing Monies out of the Treasury for services not mentioned in the Act granting the Money." Regardless of the Commons House's appeals, he added, "it shall never shake my firm Purpose of paying an exact obedience to the Instruction. . . ."[59]

Nevertheless, the Commons House attempted to convince Bull that the drawing up of the additional instruction had been based on the misconception that the lower house had disposed of funds already appropriated when it made the grant to Wilkes. It argued that the situation of South Carolina differed materially from that of England. In England all surpluses from the civil list were expressly given to the king and all other surpluses were devoted to the sinking fund, so there were no unappropriated funds. In South Carolina there were funds which were neither granted to the king nor otherwise appropriated, which "must and can only be considered as Monies of the People, and have as such, been every Year upon the Settlement of the Treasurers Accounts, applied by this House alone, either in Aid of Taxes, or to such other Purposes as they thought fit." Whenever funds which were already appropriated were diverted to another purpose, the Commons House contended, it had always asked for the concurrence of the Council and the governor.[60]

Since the Commons House could not budge Bull and the Council from their stand, it chose to let the public debt mount rather than yield to the additional instruction. The session of the Assembly came to an end without accomplishing anything about the tax bill.

At the autumn session of 1771, the Commons House attempted to hide the sum of £10,500 in the new tax bill by including it under the heading of "Extraordinary Expences" without itemizing the amounts for particular expenses.[61] The Council was too alert to be trapped. It found the item for £28,123 14s 8d and rightly suspected that the reimbursement of the public treasurer might be included under the listing of "other Services." It demanded a specific accounting. It also professed surprise that the tax bill did not contain the penalty clauses required by the additional instruction and requested that the clauses be inserted. The Commons House returned the tax bill without alteration, and the deadlock continued.[62]

Ill feelings had been mounting for some time before the rejection of the new tax bill, but that event possibly spurred the Commons House into drastic action. On October 2, 1771, it had ordered the joint public treasurers, Henry Peronneau and Benjamin Dart, to lend money to the commissioners of the silk manufacture to enable them to produce raw silk to be shipped to Great Britain.[63] This was one more attempt to exercise authority over money independently of the governor and Council. The public treasurers had not paid the money. On October 18 the Commons

House had resolved that the Treasury should receive and pay out foreign coins at current prices, meaning the higher values which had been adopted by citizens of Charles Town early in 1771.[64] The public treasurers had again refused to comply. Just after the rejection of the tax bill on November 4, the Commons House summoned both men to appear the next day to answer charges, and every member of the Commons House was ordered to appear or to be fined £5.[65] A showdown was in the making.

Speaker Peter Manigault asked the public treasurers a series of questions which revealed that no order of the Commons House prior to the order of October 2 had ever been refused by them, and that there was sufficient unappropriated money in the Treasury to pay the order. The reason given by the public treasurers for ignoring the order was that the additional instruction made payment impossible—if they had paid the order, they said, their bonds would have been forfeited. Concerning the directive to receive foreign coins, Peronneau answered that he was "bound in duty to support the Currency of the Province." Since the directive was only the opinion of the Commons House, he felt he could not honor it without the approval of the "whole legislature." Furthermore, he said, British law prohibited receiving Spanish dollars at inflated rates.

After being given time to consider whether they would pay the order, Peronneau replied that "If he thought the Privileges and Liberties of the People were at stake by his refusing to pay the Money he would do it," but since they were not, he could not risk having his bond sued upon and himself "thereby ruined." Dart replied that "he had consulted Counsel as well as many sensible People" and all agreed that payment would result in forfeiture of the bonds. The Commons House thereupon ordered the speaker to draw up warrants for the arrest of the public treasurers for contempt of the authority and privileges of the Commons House. Governor Montagu, newly returned to the province, heard of the arrests and dissolved the Assembly, thus stopping the warrants and securing the release of Peronneau and Dart.[66]

Henry Laurens, writing from England, probably expressed the sentiments of many members of the Commons House when he was surprised that Dart had refused to make the payment ("Mr

Peronneau has the Merit of acting uniformly"). "Had *he* bow'd obedience to the Ministerial Instructions—*who* was so warm in violent Oppositions to Acts of Parliament in 1765 and 1770?" Laurens believed that Dart should have resigned rather than offer the excuse of avoiding the forfeiture of his bond. "I wish he had acted when Joint Treasurer—as he would have insisted upon a Joint Treasurer to have acted—when he was a Member of the Assembly."[67]

In his opening speech to the new Assembly which met in April 1772, Governor Montagu pointedly reminded the Commons House of the reasons for dissolution of the previous Assembly— the controversy over the tax bill and the arrest of the public treasurers—and of his intended firmness in enforcing the additional instruction.[68] The Commons House, for its part, announced its intention to waste no time on bills which might prove abortive but indicated readiness to submit any bills when there was hope that they might be accepted in the "usual and Constitutional Mode," that is, without the penalty clauses required by the additional instruction. The Commons House was in effect threatening another legislative sit-down strike.[69] A few days later, after acidly commenting on the Commons House's failure to regard the public credit as sufficient inducement to proceed with business, Montagu dissolved the Assembly once more.[70]

The governor had had enough of the Commons House's obstinance. He framed a carefully calculated plan to break its will and impose control upon it. He delayed issuing writs of election until almost the end of the six-month period, the maximum legal interval between sessions. Then, in an attempt to make resistance more difficult, he summoned the Assembly to meet in Beaufort, some seventy miles to the southwest of Charles Town and far from the residences of most of the patriotic leaders.[71] The Commons House rose to the challenge, however. In previous meetings it had frequently, even usually, been unable to summon a quorum on the opening days of its sessions, even when it met in Charles Town. On opening day in Beaufort, no fewer than thirty-four members out of a total of forty-eight were in attendance.[72]

Obviously provoked at being thus thwarted, Governor Montagu did not deign to receive the Commons House until two days later, when he made a defensive speech about his right to call the Assembly to meet in Beaufort. Approaching the subject in dispute, he said that the House of Commons in England had never appropriated money without the consent of the other branches of the legislature, and therefore the Commons House of South Carolina could not do so. After a stern warning against constitutional innovation, he prorogued the Assembly to meet October 22 in Charles Town.[73]

Montagu's scheme had failed. If anything, he had strengthened the determination of the Commons House. Christopher Gadsden introduced a set of vigorous resolutions condemning Montagu's handling of the Beaufort Assembly, and Montagu in a fit of rage dissolved the Assembly when he discovered that it had continued to sit for business after it had received a message from him requiring its presence in the Council Chamber.[74]

The newly elected Commons House was no more pliable. Montagu believed that Rawlins Lowndes, who had been elected speaker when Manigault resigned because of ill health, had deliberately kept the Commons House's journals from him during the previous Assembly to deny him information about its proceedings. Now he refused to accept Lowndes as speaker, and the Commons House refused to choose anyone else. Montagu prorogued the Assembly by an irregular procedure, and to prevent complications from arising from his blunder, he dissolved the Assembly once more.[75]

DEADLOCK

Public affairs in South Carolina had been at a standstill for several years. The last tax act had been passed on August 23, 1769, and the last legislation of any sort on March 20, 1771.[76] Rather than submit to dictation on financial matters and give up the power of controlling the Treasury, the Commons House had chosen to pass no laws at all.[77] In a sense, the colonial period ended for South Carolina in 1771 rather than in 1775 or 1776. There were other motivations, but control over public funds was at the heart of the controversy that sparked revolution.

NOTES

[1]Commons House Journal, June 5, 1739, *JCH, 1736–1739*, 718–19.

[2]Commons House Journal, May 5, 1752, xxvii, Part Two, 434–40; December 7, 1752, xxviii, Part One, 86–92.

[3]*Statutes*, iii, 655.

[4]Commons House Journal, December 12, 1752, xxviii, Part One, 107–8; Miscellaneous Records, I I (or J J), 369.

[5]Commons House Journal, December 2, 1725, *Journal of the Commons House of Assembly of South Carolina, November 1, 1725–April 30, 1726*, ed. A.S. Salley (Columbia, 1945), 46; June 1, 1738, *JCH, 1736–1739*, 572; Manuscript Act 796; *Statutes*, ii, 238, 285, 378–79; iii, 10, 172; iv, 317; vii, 22.

[6]Commons House Journal, August 2, 1765, *JCH, 1765*, 158.

[7]See below, "Rejection of Money Bills."

[8]Commons House Journal, March 4, 1736/7, *JCH, 1736–1739*, 282–84.

[9]*Statutes*, iii, 340, 409.

[10]Council Journal, May 4, 1737, Public Record Office photostats in S.C. Dept. of Archives and History, i (C.O. 5/438), 59, 60.

[11]Commons House Journal, October 7, 1737, *JCH, 1736–1739*, 341.

[12]Commons House Journal, February 4, 1737/8, ibid., 470; Upper House Journal, February 4, 1737/8, CJ, vii, 65.

[13]Commons House Journal, March 11, 1737/8, *JCH, 1736–1739*, 537; Upper House Journal, March 11, 1737/8, CJ, vii, 102–3.

[14]Commons House Journal, February 16–17, 1710/11, iii, 530–31.

[15]Commons House Journal, August 22–23, 25, 1701, *JCH, August 1701*, 15–19.

[16]Commons House Journal, February 9, 1738/9, May 31, 1739, *JCH, 1736–1739*, 623–24, 710–11; November 22, 28–29, 1739, *JCH, 1739–1741*, 41–42, 57–58, 63.

[17]Commons House Journal, March 21, 1755, xxx, Part Two, 405; Ledger B, 1, 2, 12, 13, 17, 23, 25, 31, 36, 38, 45, 49.

[18]*Statutes*, ii, 68.

[19]Ibid., 305–6.

[20]Commons House Journal, April 8, 1706, *JCH, 1706*, 54–55; June 6, 1712, iv, 81–82.

[21]Commons House Journal, March 5, 1755, xxx, Part One, 319. The order was prompted largely by Jacob Motte's perennial slowness in preparing his accounts.

[22]Commons House Journal, September 20, 22, 1733, Sainsbury Copies, i, Part Two, 1135–45.

[23]Commons House Journal, March 21, 1734/5, March 25, 1735, *JCH, 1734–1735*, 123, 128–31.

[24]*Statutes*, iii, 308–17, 352–62.

[25]Commons House Journal, March 11, 13, 1751/2, xxvii, Part One, 232, 246–47.

[26]Commons House Journal, March 15, 1754, xxix, 244.

[27]Commons House Journal, February 24–25, March 5, 1736/7, *JCH, 1736–1739*, 245, 249–52, 290.

[28]Commons House Journal, March 21, 1755, xxx, Part Two, 405.

[29]Commons House Journal, April 2, 15, 21–22, 1756, xxxi, Part One, 167, 185–87, 189–92.

[30]Commons House Journal, June 25, 30, 1756, ibid., 217–18, 219–20.

[31]The 1756 controversy prompted a writer in the newspaper to propose that that power be ended by having the Council stripped of its role as Upper House of the Assembly and made a purely executive council. *South-Carolina Gazette,* May 13, 1756. Nothing came of the suggestion at the time, but it was often revived when there was a controversy about public finance.

[32]Commons House Journal, December 4, 1725, *JCH, 1725–1726,* 54–55.

[33]Commons House Journal, December 14–18, 1725, ibid., 70–76.

[34]Commons House Journal, March 28, 1735, *JCH, 1734–1735,* 151–52.

[35]Commons House Journal, April 23, 28, 1735, IX, Part One, 219–21, 257.

[36]*Statutes,* III, 448.

[37]Upper House Journal, April 4, 10, 1739, CJ, VII, 201–2, 215–16.

[38]Commons House Journal, June 5, 1739, *JCH, 1736–1739,* 720.

[39]*JCH, 1739–1741,* viii.

[40]Commons House Journal, November 27, 1739, ibid., 52.

[41]Commons House Journal, December 11, 1739, ibid., 92–93.

[42]Commons House Journal, December 11, 15, 1739, ibid., 97–98, 122.

[43]Commons House Journal, June 27–29, 1748, *JCH, 1748,* 365–68, 370–72, 376–77, 390–91.

[44]In September 1762 Boone had refused to adminsiter the oath of office of Christopher Gadsden as a member of the Commons House, on the contention that Gadsden had not been elected legally. From then until Boone's departure in May 1764 the Commons House had refused to transact normal business. See Jack P. Greene, "The Gadsden Election Controversy and the Revolutionary Movement in South Carolina," *Mississippi Valley Historical Review,* XLVI (1959), 469–92.

[45]Commons House Journal, August 22, 1764, XXXVI, 244.

[46]Commons House Journal, August 23, 1764, ibid., 245–47. The Commons House did not pass the resolution, preferring instead simply to return the tax bill, but the resolution was not expunged from the minutes.

[47]Commons House Journal, October 3–4, 1764, ibid., 266–68.

[48]Commons House Journal, June 17, 20, 1766, XXXVII, Part One, 2d pagination, 160–62, 164–66.

[49]For a fuller account of the controversy, see Jack P. Greene, "Bridge to Revolution: The Wilkes Fund Controversy in South Carolina, 1769–1755," *Journal of Southern History,* XXIX (1963), 19–52.

[50]Commons House Journal, December 8, 1769, XXXVIII, Part Two, 215.

[51]Peter Manigault et al. to Robert Morris, December 9, 1769, "Garth Correspondence," ed. Joseph W. Barnwell, *South Carolina Historical and Genealogical Magazine,* XXXI (1930), 132–34.

[52]Wilkes had been celebrated as a hero in South Carolina as early as October 1768, when a parade from the "Tree of Liberty" to Dillon's Tavern had featured the number forty-five. *South Carolina Gazette; and Country Journal,* October 4, 1768.

[53]Commons House Journal, April 7, 9, 1770, XXXVIII, Part Two, 382, 386–87.

[54]Commons House Journal, April 10–11, 1770, ibid., 390–91, 393.

[55]Commons House Journal, June 5, 1770, ibid., 393–95.

[56]Commons House Journal, July 23, 1770, ibid., 395–96.

[57]Commons House Journal, August 16, 1770, ibid., 403–5; enclosure with Board of Trade to Committee of Privy Council for Plantation Affairs, April 4, 1770, Sainsbury Transcripts, XXXII, 236–40.

[58]Commons House Journal, September 7,1770, xxxviii, Part Two, 453.

[59]Commons House Journal, January 31, February 7, 1771, ibid., Part Three, 474, 476.

[60]Commons House Journal, February 26, 1771, ibid., 497–99.

[61]Commons House Journal, October 16, 1771, ibid., 563.

[62]Commons House Journal, November 4, 1771, ibid., 577–78. The journal heading reads incorrectly, "Monday the 4th. day of November 1772."

[63]Commons House Journal, October 2, 1771, ibid., 543.

[64]Commons House Journal, October 18, 1771, ibid., 565; Peter Manigault to Daniel Blake, March 10, 1771, "Letterbook of Peter Manigault, 1763–1773," ed. Maurice A. Crouse, *South Carolina Historical Magazine*, LXX (1969), 188.

[65]Commons House Journal, November 4, 1771, xxxviii, Part Three, 579.

[66]Commons House Journal, November 5, 1771, ibid., 580–84.

[67]Henry Laurens to John Lewis Gervais, December 28, 1771, Letterbook 1771–1772, 143–44, Henry Laurens Papers, South Carolina Historical Society.

[68]Commons House Journal, April 3, 1772, C.O. 5/478, 3–4.

[69]Commons House Journal, April 7, 1772, ibid., 4–6.

[70]Commons House Journal, April 10, 1772, ibid., 11.

[71]Commons House Journal, October 8, 1772, xxxix, 1st pagination, 1.

[72]Commons House Journal, October 8, 1772, ibid., 1–2.

[73]Commons House Journal, October 10, 1772, ibid., 4–6.

[74]Commons House Journal, October 29–30, November 10, 1772, ibid., 20–24, 27–29.

[75]Charles Greville Montagu to Earl of Dartmouth, January 21, 1773, Sainsbury Transcripts, xxxiii, 204–5.

[76]*Statutes*, IV, 315, 331.

[77]The only legislation passed after 1771 was an act which revived or extended existing laws and another which sought to prevent counterfeiting of the currency of neighboring provinces, both passed March 4, 1775. *Statutes*, IV, 331–36.

CHAPTER VII

The Final Years

THE FINAL YEARS of the Public Treasury of South Carolina were filled with financial crises and constant bickering between the two houses of the Assembly, culminating in a paralysis of the constituted government and the assumption of governmental power by a revolutionary regime.

MOUNTING FINANCIAL CRISES

A financial crisis had been building since 1770, when the tax bill had first been rejected by the Council. Only the continuing revenues from the import and export duties kept the Treasury going at all. Early in 1773 the Commons House stubbornly prepared a new tax bill without the required penalty clauses, and the Council stubbornly refused to accept it.[1] Gravely concerned about the state of the public credit and convinced that the Commons House would never provide a tax bill which would comply with the royal instruction, the Council in August 1773 summoned Henry Peronneau to give an accounting of the Treasury. Peronneau presented a very gloomy report. Motte's estate still owed £63,974 19s 5d on the deficit which Motte had incurred as public treasurer. Because of the acute shortage of currency, merchants had been unable to pay their import duties in cash and had given bonds for £127,674 6s 11d which had not been collected and probably could not be collected soon. Peronneau said there was not over £10,000 in the Treasury, and "he was really Apprehensive of a Public Bankruptcy and being obliged to stop payment, if the Public Debts were not more punctually discharged." He estimated that with current funds the Treasury could continue operations only until October 1. When asked how much revenue would be needed for the next six months, he replied that he would require about £50,000. The Council then addressed an appeal to Lieutenant Governor Bull, desiring him to order the recovery of the balance due from Motte's estate, to compel the payment of £50,000 from the merchants who had been longest in debt to the province for payment of duties and to direct the attorney-general to take steps to force the payment of the remaining sums.[2]

The Council had, perhaps unwittingly, touched off a new round in the political war. Bull, who was already worried by his poor relations with the Commons House, now bristled at the attempt of the Council to dictate policy to him without his asking for its advice. Bull answered the Council's letter in cool tones, saying that he would take whatever steps seemed necessary to him. Surprised at this reaction from the lieutenant governor, the Council passed several resolutions defending its actions as proper and respectful, and maintaining that it was "not only the undoubted right but it is the indispensible Duty of this House at all times to Examine into the state of the Public Treasury and to Address, Counsell and Advise the Governor in every matter relative thereto, which shall appear to this House to be conducive to the Public Credit and Honor and to the safety and Protection of the Public Treasure."[3]

The Commons House also reacted vigorously to the Council's actions. An investigating committee reported that the general situation was far from being as serious as the Council maintained. It insisted that the £127,674 6s 11d due from "Gentlemen in Trade" should be regarded as actually in the Treasury, in addition to £10,000 in gold and silver and various other sums in old torn bills, tax certificates, public orders, and other forms of currency. Moreover, some £38,000 more would soon be due from the merchants. There seemed, therefore, to be no occasion for the Council's alarm that the Treasury must shortly stop payment. In adopting the committee's recommendations, the Commons House condemned the public treasurers as being "too officious and busy, in misrepresenting the state of the Treasury to the Council," and the Council as acting in a way that was unprecedented, hasty, disrespectful to the Commons House, and actually unlawful.[4]

The Council retorted that the Commons House was being unrealistic. The £127,674 6s 11d was not in the Treasury and could not be produced by the public treasurers, since it was tied up in the bonds which the merchants had given instead of cash. The Council was inclined to blame the predicament on the public treasurers themselves. It passed a resolution that the practice of allowing public funds to remain in private hands for private gain was "a gross perversion of the Public Treasury, and a sore and dangerous evil by means whereof the Treasury of this Province is kept in a state of Beggary and want and in a total Incapacity to answer any unforeseen demands which the Wisdom of the Legislature may see proper on any great and sudden Emergency." It urged that the practice be stopped as soon as possible.[5]

As it had done in 1771, the Commons House then determined to bring the public treasurers before it to stand scrutiny, setting September 2, 1773, as the date.[6] Before the time arrived, however, the political situation had deteriorated seriously. First came word that the Council had refused to give a third reading to a bill to prevent counterfeiting of the currencies of neighboring provinces, a measure which the Commons House deemed essential.[7] William Henry Drayton, a member of the Council whose disgust at the domination of that body by placemen from England had been growing for some time, protested that the public would soon lose all faith in the Council. He caused a portion of the Council's minutes to be printed in the *South-Carolina Gazette,* whereupon one of the publishers was imprisoned by the Council for contempt. He was, however, released on a writ of *habeas corpus* on the order of two justices of the peace who happened also to be members of the Commons House (one was Speaker Rawlins Lowndes). There was a furious embroilment over the affair, and though it had no direct connection with the Treasury, it distracted both houses of the Assembly while it was going on.[8]

Then the Commons House created another controversy by

refusing to provide reimbursement to the public treasurers for having paid £30,882 12s 4d for the salaries of judges and the attorney-general during the period February 19, 1770, to May 19, 1772, the interval between the proclamation of the approval of the Circuit Court Act of 1769 and the completion of the court-houses and jails which were authorized by it. The Commons House maintained that the act did not intend for the salaries to commence until the courthouses and jails were ready for use by the officials.[9]

Unfortunately, the Commons House journals do not explain what sort of examination Peronneau and Dart underwent when they appeared before the Commons House, other than that they were questioned about what authority they had for having paid the salaries. In all likelihood, the public treasurers were asked to give full obedience to the Commons House alone, for the next day, seemingly as a test, they were ordered to pay £1,500 to the commissary-general to provide transportation to the backcountry for recently arrived poor Irish Protestants. The order was not sent to the Council for its concurrence.[10]

Because of its involvement in the Drayton episode, the Commons House did not come to a resolution on the public treasurers until September 9, when it laid the blame for the province's financial ills at their feet. Then, agreeing with the Council that private gain on their part was not to be tolerated, the Commons House resolved to deprive the public treasurers of any advantage they might have gained by charging them interest on the bonds and notes on which they themselves were receiving interest from the merchants.[11]

Just before it received permission to adjourn for several months, the Commons House resolved that if the sum due from former Public Treasurer Jacob Motte's estate were not fully paid within three months, the attorney-general should sue on the bonds which Motte had posted.[12] Because of a prorogation, the Assembly did not meet again until March 1774, at which time Lieutenant Governor Bull sent the Commons House a copy of a letter which Attorney-General Egerton Leigh had recently written him. Leigh complained of the difficulty of following the Commons House's order to sue on Motte's bonds. He noted first that there were twenty-six bonds involved and that it would be very difficult to frame a writ which would agree with the wording of all of them; he warned that "a variance may be fatal." Second, the total penalties covered by the bonds amounted to only £49,140, but Motte's estate still owed £61,474 19s 5d. If the bonds were put in suit, no more than £49,140 could ever be recovered. He thought it advisable, therefore, that he sue the executors of the estate for the entire amount and let the bonds stand as collateral security.[13]

The Commons House was unimpressed by Leigh's points. It saw no difficulty in framing a writ, and it maintained that suing on the bonds would be entirely satisfactory. If Motte's estate were credited with the £10,500 still due it from the public for the money sent to John Wilkes, the amount owed would be only £48,974 19s 5d, or somewhat less than the penal sum of the bonds. This interpretation would signify victory for the Commons House in the long-standing Wilkes controversy, and it was not accepted. Bull instructed Leigh to sue Motte's estate.[14]

Shortly afterward, the Commons House hit upon an expedient means to solve some of the province's financial difficulties. Since the Council had prevented tax bills from passing for the last four years, the Commons House resolved that it would attempt to alleviate the distress of public creditors by placing tax certificates in their hands *before* a tax law was enacted. (One of the major factors in the distress was the scarcity of currency, and it will be remembered that tax certificates formed a substantial part of the currency.) Public creditors would be given certificates representing their indebtedness and the interest on the amounts which had accumulated since the payments were due. The certificates were to be issued by the authority of the Commons House and signed by five of its members. They would be paid out of the proceeds of the next taxation law, whenever there should be one.[15] The certificates were eagerly accepted as currency by nearly everyone in the province.[16] Because the issue was so popular, a similar issue was authorized June 1, 1775, to pay for the public debts that had been incurred since the first issue.[17]

THE END OF THE PUBLIC TREASURY

As the inactivity of the General Assembly of South Carolina continued, actual powers of government began to be assumed by the "general meetings" which were held to express sentiment for Massachusetts and its resistance to the Intolerable Acts. The Commons House was not fundamentally opposed to the irregular group. It even agreed to provide for the expenses of the delegates who were selected by the general meeting of July 6–8, 1774, to attend the First Continental Congress in Philadelphia in September.[18]

By the time that the new Governor, Lord William Campbell, arrived in Charles Town on June 18, 1775, the constituted government of the province had practically come to an end. The first Provincial Congress had already met; the association had been formed to enforce obedience to the nonimportation, nonexportation, and nonconsumption agreements drafted at Philadelphia; troops had been raised to go to the aid of Boston; the powder and arms of the province had been confiscated by the patriots; a council of safety had been established; and the revolutionary regime had taken steps to supersede the Public Treasury.[19]

By a resolution passed four days before Campbell arrived, the Provincial Congress had created the office of the commissioners of the treasury, which would operate under the direction of the council of safety and issue the bills of credit for £1,000,000 which were authorized by the same resolution. The next day the Congress named John Neufville, William Gibbes, and Peter Bacot to be the commissioners.[20] Thereafter the Congress called upon either the joint public treasurers or the commissioners of the treasury to make reports, depending upon which funds were involved.[21]

Again, the Commons House was not hostile to the revolutionary legislature. It noted that during the recess of the General Assembly, the people of the province had been "apprehensive of instigated Insurrections of Slaves, and Depredations from Indians and others," and that the Provincial Congress had raised two regiments of foot troops and a regiment of rangers to deal with the problem. The Commons House voted unanimously to provide for calling in and sinking the issue of £1,000,000 which had been made by the Provincial Congress, but there is no indication that any such steps were ever actually taken.[22] Despite Governor Campbell's plea that the Commons House "make a Constitutional Provision for the Public Debts," the Commons House transacted almost no business of consequence. After August 30, 1775, it ceased altogether to hold sessions, and on September 15, 1775, Campbell dissolved the Assembly because of its inactivity.[23] It never met again.

The Public Treasury continued to exist, however, alongside the treasury presided over by the commissioners of the treasury. Such an arrangement could hardly have continued for long. Toward the end of February 1776, a member of the Provincial Congress paid a visit to Peronneau to ask him if he would obey the orders of the Congress insofar as they related to the Treasury. On March 6, 1776, Peronneau and Dart were presented with a letter from William Henry Drayton, president of the Provincial Congress, which read, "GENTLEMEN, YOU are hereby prohibited from issuing or causing to be issued, any public money in your charge, without order first had and obtained from the Congress, or proper authority derived from them."[24]

The commissioners of the treasury had become by far the more important officials, disbursing the £1,000,000 issue and then the succeeding issues of £120,000 and £750,000 authorized by the Provincial Congress.[25] During the period January 1, 1775–March 4, 1776, the public treasurers disbursed only £22,408 8s 2d.[26]

The Constitution of South Carolina, adopted March 26, 1776, stipulated "That Commissioners of the Treasury, . . . be chosen by the General Assembly and Legislative Council jointly by ballot, and commissioned by the President and Commander in Chief, during good behaviour; but shall be removed on address of the General Assembly and Legislative Council."[27] The powers of the council of safety were transferred to the president and commander-in-chief, John Rutledge, by an act of April 6, 1776. Three days later the General Assembly and Legislative Council repealed the appointment of Peronneau and Dart as joint public treasurers and turned over the Treasury completely to the new commissioners of the treasury, Gideon Dupont, Roger Smith, and George Abbott Hall.[28] A new era in public finance was beginning.

NOTES

[1]Commons House Journal, March 27, 1773, XXXIX, 2d pagination, 23.
[2]Upper House Journal, August 11, 1773, C.O. 5/478, 6–7.
[3]Upper House Journal, August 14, 1773, ibid., 9.
[4]Commons House Journal, August 18–19, 1773, XXXIX, 2d pagination, 48–49, 51–52.
[5]Upper House Journal, August 24, 1773, C.O. 5/478, 13–14.
[6]Commons House Journal, August 26, 1773, XXXIX, 2d pagination, 64.
[7]Commons House Journal, August 27, 1773, ibid., 65.
[8]See Smith, *South Carolina as a Royal Province*, 388–402.
[9]Commons House Journal, September 1, 1773, XXXIX, 2d pagination, 69.
[10]Commons House Journal, September 2–3, 1773, ibid., 73–74, 76.
[11]Commons House Journal, September 9–10, 1773, ibid., 90–91. It is not certain that the step was actually taken. Possibly this is the occasion that Peronneau recollected as having occurred in 1771, out of which nothing resulted. Loyalist Transcripts, LII, 531–32.
[12]Commons House Journal, September 10, 1773, XXXIX, 2d pagination, 92.
[13]Commons House Journal, March 3, 1774, ibid., 105–6.
[14]Commons House Journal, March 10–11, 1774, ibid., 115, 118.
[15]Commons House Journal, March 24, 1774, ibid., 162–64.
[16]William Bull to Earl of Dartmouth, May 3, 1774, Sainsbury Transcripts, XXXIV, 36–40.
[17]Commons House Journal, June 1, 1775, XXXIX, 2d pagination, 287.
[18]David D. Wallace, *South Carolina, A Short History, 1520–1948* (Chapel Hill, 1951; Columbia, 1961), 253–54; Commons House Journal, August 2, 1774, XXXIX, 2d pagination, 173. The Commons House did not attempt to get the money from the public treasurer, however; it offered interest to any person who would loan the funds.
[19]Wallace, *Short History*, 255–59.
[20]Provincial Congress Journal, June 14–15, 1775, *JPC, 1775–1776*, 50–51, 53.
[21]Provincial Congress Journal, November 1, 3, 15, 18, 1775; March 5–6, 1776, *JPC, 1775–1776*, 84, 88, 131, 134, 222, 224.
[22]Commons House Journal, July 12, 1775, XXXIX, 2d pagination, 295.
[23]Commons House Journal, July 29, August 30, September 15, 1775, ibid., 305, 314.
[24]Provincial Congress Journal, March 6,1776, *JPC, 1775–1776*, 226; Loyalist Transcripts, LII, 518–19.
[25]Provincial Congress Journal, November 15, 1775, March 6, 1776,*JPC, 1775–1776*, 130, 225.
[26]Publick's Ledger, 1771–1776, 14.
[27]Provincial Congress Journal, March 26, 1776,*JPC, 1775–1776*, 261–62.
[28]Loyalist Transcripts, LII, 518–19; *Statutes*, IV, 336–38, 342–43.

Bibliographical Notes

The secondary sources to which the student of the Public Treasury of colonial South Carolina may turn for information are few and of varying quality. Most of them concentrate on the political issues involved in control of finance and appointments and give little attention to the technical operations of the Treasury.

Several general works shed some light on the subject. Two volumes of Edward McCrady's four-volume history of South Carolina deal with the colonial period: *The History of South Carolina under the Proprietary Government, 1670–1719* (New York, 1897), and *The History of South Carolina under the Royal Government, 1719–1776* (New York, 1899). Both are cast in a rather rigid chronological format. David Duncan Wallace's *The History of South Carolina*, 4 vols. (New York, 1934–35), and *South Carolina, A Short History, 1520–1948* (Chapel Hill, 1951; Columbia, 1961), are freer in form but are still essentially narratives.

To garner anything substantial the reader will need to consult specialized works. Two early students of South Carolina's colonial government made contributions that have been largely superseded by the work of later scholars. Both Edson L. Whitney, *The Government of the Colony of South Carolina* (Baltimore, 1895), and David Duncan Wallace, *Constitutional History of South Carolina from 1725–1775* (Abbeville, S.C., 1899), are tentative efforts at best on the subject of the Public Treasury, but they will serve as a quick introduction. Unfortunately, Whitney can be very misleading at times. Easily the most valuable early work on the Public Treasury is contained in W. Roy Smith, *South Carolina as a Royal Province* (New York, 1903). Smith was thorough in his research, and I have found that his conclusions about public finance are generally still valid. Jack P. Greene, *The Quest for Power: The Lower Houses of Assembly in the Southern Royal Colonies, 1689–1776* (Chapel Hill, 1963), makes a fine contribution to the study of the political issues involved in the struggle for control of the Public Treasury. M. Eugene Sirmans, *Colonial South Carolina, A Political History, 1663–1763* (Chapel Hill, 1966), is of mixed value. It has little on the operation of the Public Treasury (and some of that is mistaken), but it is very useful for the insights which it gives into the political setting within which the Public Treasury operated.

Joseph Albert Ernst, *Money and Politics in America, 1755–1775* (Chapel Hill, 1973), deals generally with the attempts by imperial authorities to control colonial currency issues and has several sections that set South Carolina within that context.

I first began wrestling with the complexities of South Carolina's public finances in "The Manigault Family of South Carolina, 1685–1783" (Ph.D. dissertation, Northwestern University, 1964), because Gabriel Manigault was public treasurer from 1735 to 1743. I have incorporated much of that research into the present work. I have also benefited from the research done by Cynthia J. Hawes in "The Beginnings of the Revenue Offices in South Carolina, to 1735" (Master's thesis, Memphis State University, 1967), part of which dealt with the Public Treasury.

However, there is no substitute for the primary sources. Although some have perished, there are enough surviving public records to give a fairly coherent picture of the Public Treasury, especially during the latter half of its existence. The most pertinent records are those prepared by the various public treasurers themselves. The South Carolina Department of Archives and History, Columbia, S.C., holds three journals covering the period 1735–76, three ledgers for 1725–30 and 1735–76, and a record of general tax receipts and payments for 1761–71, and it has published them in a convenient microfilm format for those who cannot visit the archives for research. The records are perhaps not as informative as they could be for an economic historian—the journals, for example, do not list the cargoes on which duties were paid—but they are usually adequate for one to gain an understanding of how the Public Treasury worked.

The journals of the Commons House, the upper house, the Council, and the Provincial Congress are also very important. Sometimes the journals are too formal to reveal much, but they often contain verbatim texts of documents that figured in controversies over the Public Treasury, and they always record the resolutions that were passed. Between the copies in the Archives and the British Public Record Office there are practically complete journals of the Commons House from 1692 to 1774; of the upper house from 1721 to 1759, late 1762 to late 1768, and late 1769 to early 1771; and of the Council from 1721 to 1775. Copies of most of the extant journals are available on microfilm from the Library of Congress in the Early State Records Project or the British Manuscripts Project; the others may be obtained from the South Carolina Department of Archives and History.

A fair number of the Commons House journals have been published. The Historical Commission of South Carolina between 1907 and 1949 published twenty-two volumes edited by A.S. Salley, all but two of which were for 1727 or earlier years. The volumes are useful, but I have not always found them to be literal transcripts of the original. From 1951 to 1962 the South Carolina Archives Department and Commission published nine volumes covering the years 1736–50, which were very well edited by J.H. Easterby and Ruth S. Green. Excellent guides to the various journals and the various states in which they may be consulted—originals, copies, transcripts, microfilms, published volumes—have been prepared by Charles E. Lee and Ruth S. Green and published in the *South Carolina Historical Magazine*, LXVII (1966), 187–202, and LXVIII (1967), 1–13, 85–96, and 165–83. The journals of the Provincial Congress were reprinted in 1960 by the Archives in a modern edition by W. Edwin Hemphill and Wylma Anne Wates from extracts published by Peter Timothy in 1775 and 1776.

The texts of most of the laws which related to the Public Treasury may be found conveniently in *The Statutes-at-Large of South Carolina*, ed. Thomas Cooper and David J. McCord, 10 vols. (Columbia, 1836–41). But the student of the Public Treasury will frequently need to resort to the manuscript acts which are filed at the Archives to supplement the printed laws, because Cooper and

McCord omitted many acts. Many of the annual tax acts were left out because of their great similarity to other acts which were printed. Some other acts were promised for later volumes and then apparently forgotten. Some were said "not now to be found." Of the latter, despite the editors' statement, many may now easily be found among the manuscript acts.

Valuable correspondence of the governors of South Carolina to the Board of Trade and the secretary of state is often found in "Records in the British Public Record Office Relating to South Carolina, 1663–1782," thirty-six volumes of handwritten transcripts prepared under the direction of W. Noel Sainsbury and located in the Archives. The same material may, of course, be found in the British Public Record Office or in the microfilms of the British Manuscripts Project from the Library of Congress, but I have used the "Sainsbury Transcripts" because of their convenience. The first five volumes were issued in facsimile by the Historical Commission of South Carolina from 1928 to 1947; the remaining volumes may be obtained on microfilm from the Archives.

The newspapers, notably the *South-Carolina Gazette,* contain more information about the Public Treasury than one might suspect. Files of the six newspapers published in South Carolina from 1732 to 1782 exist in many areas, but the most convenient source is the microfilm edition prepared by the Charleston Library Society.

I found private manuscripts to be of little value for this study. Only the Henry Laurens Papers, located in the South Carolina Historical Society, offered more than a scattering of pertinent items.

INDEX